*This book belongs to*

Mrs Madeline Mitchell
284 Little Machias Rd
Cutler ME 04626-3148

B.294

# SIMPLIFY
# YOUR
# CHRISTMAS

❄

· ALSO BY ELAINE ST. JAMES ·

*Simplify Your Life*

*Inner Simplicity*

*Living the Simple Life*

*Simplify Your Life with Kids*

❄

# SIMPLIFY
# YOUR
# CHRISTMAS

*100 Ways to Reduce the Stress and
Recapture the Joy of the Holidays*

## ELAINE ST. JAMES

**Andrews McMeel
Publishing**

Kansas City

www.andrewsmcmeel.com

98  99  00  01  02  RDC  10  9  8  7  6  5  4

Library of Congress Cataloging-in-Publication Data

St. James, Elaine.
Simplify your Christmas : 100 ways to reduce the stress and recapture the joy of the holidays / Elaine St. James.
p.   cm.
ISBN 0–8362–6785–0
1. Christmas—United States.   2. Simplicity.
3. Stress management—United States.   I. Title.
GT4986.A1S7   1998
394.2663—dc21
98–23467
CIP

ATTENTION: SCHOOLS AND BUSINESSES

Andrews McMeel books are available at quantity discounts with bulk purchase for educational, business, or sales promotional use. For information, please write to: Special Sales Department, Andrews McMeel Publishing, 4520 Main Street, Kansas City, Missouri  64111.

*· To Jane Dystel ·*

# · *Contents* ·

## Two: DISMANTLING CHRISTMAS PAST

## Three: CREATING A NEW APPROACH

## Four: CHRISTMAS CARDS

## Five: KIDS AND CHRISTMAS

## Contents

### Six: GIFT GIVING

### Seven: DECKING THE HALLS

## *Eight: COOKING THE GOOSE*

## *Nine: MAKING MERRY*

Contents

### Ten: HOLIDAY SPENDING

### Eleven: A VERY SIMPLE CHRISTMAS

# · *Acknowledgments* ·

I'D LIKE TO CONVEY a very special thank-you to my friend and agent, Jane Dystel, whose idea it was to write this book, and to her staff, Miriam Goderich, Susanna Kirk, Jonas Ashkenazi, Cindy Day, and Alexandra Sullivan for their ongoing support and great ideas.

I'm deeply indebted to Catherine Whitney for her assistance, patience, and perseverance, and to Catha Paquette for having a sharp pencil, an eagle eye, and the honesty to call them as she sees them. I am also indebted to Joe Phillips for his unstinting efforts to keep me up to date in the world of technology.

Scott Hamilton's inspiration has been invaluable, as has been the friendship and encouragement of Pat Rushton, Carolyn Howe, Beverly Brennan, Judy Babcock, Felix Fusco, and Barbara Henricks.

I'm immensely grateful to my aunt, Kathleen Schiffler;

and my cousins Joanie Nicholas, Ellen Horsch, Karin Kirk, Mark Schiffler, Kathie Myers, and their spouses and kids; and to our own kids, Michelle, Bill, Jessie, Megan, Lisa, and Eric, for their love and their presence in my life. Thank you all for setting the example.

I'm also thankful to everyone at Andrews McMeel, most especially for the editorial guidance of Chris Schillig, Tom Thornton, Jake Morrissey, and Jean Zevnik; the efficient assistance of JuJu Johnson, Eden Thorne, and Shannon Guder; and the artistic acuity of Tim Lynch.

I couldn't have written this book without the generosity of Henriette Klauser, Vera Cole, Seanna Beck, Amie Liebeskind, Kim Isztwan, Karen Baker, Cynthia Wright, Martha Roberts, Gail De Ri, Janet Wilson, Patti Marshall, and all the other readers, friends, and strangers who shared their stories and ideas for simplifying the holidays.

And, as always, I'm grateful to my husband, Wolcott Gibbs Jr., for everything.

> *"Last year I woke up the day after Christmas
> and I was so tired I just wanted to cry."*
>
> —A YOUNG MOTHER OF TWO FROM BOSTON

THIS BOOK IS WRITTEN for everyone who loves Christmas but is tired of the stress and exhaustion that has become an integral part of the holidays.

When I wrote *Simplify Your Life*, I suggested that if you didn't like the holidays, you could bow out. That's what my husband, Gibbs, and I did when we decided to simplify our lives. This was a gradual process that took us several years.

First we discontinued our tradition of decorating the tree—mostly because our cats found a fully trimmed tree an irresistible playground that quickly turned into pandemonium.

We then stopped giving each other gifts, and halted the gift exchange with family and friends—except for the younger kids in our lives who still believed in Santa. In our process of clearing out, it seemed pointless to continue a tradition that brought more stuff back into our lives.

And we decided not to participate in the Christmas dinner, mostly because it was too much of an extravaganza.

The holidays have become a joyous season for us, and one we both look forward to. They're an interval of quiet reflection and retreat from the busy world. They're a time when we can easily continue connecting with Mother Earth and the seasons, and giving back to the community we live in. And they've become a powerfully spiritual interlude when, in the silence and simplicity, we can unite with each other and with our own souls.

But even though I've heard from others who've bowed out, too, eliminating the holiday celebrations completely is too drastic a step for most people. Many readers have said, "Wait a minute! I don't want to stop celebrating Christmas altogether—I just want to make it easier. How can I do that?"

So I took the basic precepts I learned from my process of simplifying and applied them to the most complicated season of the year. This book is not about celebrating Christmas the old-fashioned way. It's about shifting our approach so the holidays are about ease, togetherness, and giving from our hearts rather than from our pocketbooks. It incorporates suggestions from scores of readers and friends who've shared their thoughts about making the holidays simpler and more meaningful.

In these pages you'll find well over a hundred ways to reduce the stress and recapture the joy of Christmas. You'll find that incorporating just one or two of these ideas will dramatically improve the way you feel about the holidays. Or you may take an entirely new approach to the way you and your family celebrate them. I hope you'll see that the possibilities for creating a simple yet truly memorable season are unlimited. That's the good news.

And there's more good news: You don't have to do it all. If you learn to make good choices, and keep those choices to a minimum, you can have your Christmas and enjoy it, too.

*One*

# GETTING
# STARTED

❄

## Remember What You Once Loved
## About the Holidays

ONE OF THE FIRST STEPS you can take to simplify Christmas is to rediscover the things you truly love about the holidays. When you take a close look, you'll see that those things don't take huge amounts of time or cost a lot of money.

To jog your memory, ask friends and family and even strangers to recall what they loved most about Christmas when they were kids. You'll find the most cherished memories are of simple pleasures. We remember sights, sounds, smells, tastes, feelings, and favorite moments like these:

"The fresh scent of pine when we first brought the Christmas tree into the house."

"Being up to my elbows in fudge while I helped Mom make Christmas candy."

"Eating peppermint ice cream and drinking eggnog by the fire."

"Drawing straws with my brother to see who got to put out the cookies and milk for Santa."

"Dad standing on a ladder trying to put the angel on the top of the tree. No matter what he did it was always crooked."

"The annual trek to pick out the perfect tree."

"Eating all the mashed potatoes and gravy I wanted."

"Going out for a drive on Christmas Eve to look at the lights on all the houses."

"Walking to midnight services with my parents. The cold air, the stars, how special it felt to be staying up so late."

"Dad getting out his telescope on Christmas Eve so we could search the sky for Santa's sleigh."

"Sitting in the dark with only the Christmas tree lights blinking, listening to Christmas carols on the radio."

"The thrill I felt of hoping to catch Santa coming down the chimney and trying to figure out how he could do it with that big bag of toys."

"Putting the baby Jesus in the crèche on Christmas Eve. I was the youngest, so I always got to do it."

"The wonderful spirit of fun and camaraderie we felt when the neighbors gathered to watch and cheer as Mr. Voss installed the lighted reindeer on his roof."

Before you rush into the holiday season, take a few moments to recollect your own favorite Christmas memories. Mr. Voss probably isn't around—though his replacement might be—but practically anything listed here (and no doubt many of your own favorites) can be adapted to your present circumstances.

Creating new holiday experiences around a few things you and your family love will go a long way toward simplifying Christmas. Just don't try to incorporate *all* the things you love.

## *Figure Out What You Don't Like*

FOR MANY PEOPLE, the holidays are a burden. The obligations, the guilt, and the exhaustion of the season far outweigh the pleasures.

"It's become too commercial" tops most people's list of what they don't like about Christmas today.

This is followed by "It's so stressful."

Then, "It's so time-consuming. It starts the day after Thanksgiving or even sooner, and continues through New Year's."

Your own list might include some of the following:

"Christmas cards: trying to write a personal message to people I haven't seen or spoken with in years."

"Standing in line—at the post office, the supermarket, the department store, the bank—everywhere."

"Kids with the gimmees."

"Spending Christmas Eve in an airport with thousands of tired, cranky, sullen people."

"The office Christmas party."

"Getting on the scales on January 2 and finding I've gained eight pounds."

"Television Christmas commericals, especially for kids' toys. They're dopey, demeaning, demoralizing, and relentless."

"The bills that come due in January!"

"The annual struggle of feeling I should want to have dinner with my family but knowing in my heart that I'd like to avoid it."

"That terrible feeling of bloat from overeating."

"Christmas music in department stores in September."

"Having to express appreciation for gifts I don't like."

"Returning gifts I don't want."

"That sinking feeling on December 26, when I wake up thinking that, in spite of all I did, it still wasn't enough."

If you feel you must change the way you celebrate Christmas, perhaps it's time to figure out what you don't like. Then exclude as many of those things as you can.

This is such a basic concept—but sometimes our lives get so hectic we forget about the basics. If you eliminated even one or two things that make the holidays stressful, the whole season would be so much more enjoyable.

## · 3 ·

## *Stop Trying to Get Organized*

"I'LL TELL YOU HOW I simplify Christmas," a reader told me at a recent speaking engagement. "Instead of getting all stressed out in November and December, I shop for gifts all year round. Every time I come across something a person on my list might like, I buy it and put it away in a closet."

I have to say that her scheme didn't sound that simple to me. Rather than shopping for only two months, Christmas consumed her time and energy throughout the entire year. As we discussed it further, she began to see my point. She admitted that she would tuck gifts away here and there, then forget where she'd put them.

Often, when it came time to wrap something she'd picked out earlier, it suddenly didn't seem to be the right thing. So she'd rush out in the last weeks before Christmas to buy something else. Then she didn't know what to do with all the gifts she'd bought that weren't right. They were cluttering up her house—and her life.

Another woman told me she started early in November baking cookies and pies and making candy, which she would then freeze so she wouldn't have to cram all the preparations into the last few days before Christmas. But unless you truly love to cook, is spreading the same load over a longer period of time any easier? And isn't it time to question the idea that we need mounds of homemade cookies, candy, and other delicacies in order to make the holidays authentic?

Simplifying the holidays is not the same thing as organizing them. When you organize, you're just reshuffling the same heavy load. When you simplify, you actually *eliminate* a large chunk of it. Simplifying is not about learning how to do more in less time. It's about doing less so you'll enjoy it more. And it's about doing less so you'll have more time. That's what we all want.

## Keep Your Blinders On

YOU DON'T HAVE TO LOOK any further than your super-market checkout stand to find one of the major tools that churn the Christmas machine and make the holidays stressful: women's magazines. Their endless advertising hype complicates the holidays more than any other factor in our culture.

Headlines shout at us in bold letters of red, green, and gold: *Stage a Gingerbread House Party! . . . Easy Etched Glass Ornaments . . . 40 Gifts to Make in an Evening . . . 100 Festive and Easy Recipes . . . Victorian Christmas Feasts . . . Make Your Own Poinsettia Stenciled Tablecloth . . . How to Decorate Christmas Cookies Like a Pro . . . 180 Ways to Make Yours a Holiday Home . . . Fast, Fabulous Last-Minute Gifts . . . 250 Shopping Ideas . . . 50 Pages of Holiday Joy! . . . Food, Gifts, Wreaths, Trims, Recipes, Party Clothes, 30-Day Holiday Countdown.*

It takes great effort to ignore these messages. They're woven into our cultural fabric so we're not even aware of them. Even if you work full-time and have three kids, you feel Grinch-like deciding not to spend the week building a gingerbread house with bay windows on four sides.

The magazines deceive us with words like *easy, simple, quick*. Just looking at the glossy photos can be overwhelming. The cover blurbs make you feel you're nowhere near as clever and creative as you'd like to be—or as the articles suggest you should be.

If you subscribe to any of these magazines, don't read them during the holiday season. Start with the September issues and toss them, covers down, directly into your recycling bin. Never, ever buy one of those magazines at the checkout stand. Don't even look at them, unless you can do so with detached amusement at the absurdities their headlines offer.

If you're longing for a simpler Christmas, it's time to challenge the belief that the holidays are about crafting decorations for every room of the house, loading tables with foods that aren't on your diet, and shopping for—or hand-making—gifts of questionable value for everyone you know and many people you don't.

## *Monitor Your Stress Levels:*
## *No, It's Not Okay to Drive*
## *and Eat Lunch at the Same Time*

I DID AN INTERVIEW with a radio talk-show host who told me that Christmas is the most hectic time of the year for her family. With two active preteens and a heavy work schedule, she's always doubling up on activities just to get everything done.

In the weeks before Christmas, she races madly from item to item on her "to do" list. She often doesn't have time to stop for lunch and finds herself driving and eating at the same time. She admitted this happened only during the holidays, and wondered if it was okay.

The sister-in-law of a friend is married and has three young children, and she and her husband both work full-time. She insists on preparing the family Christmas dinner for twenty-five by herself. She spends weeks baking, cleaning, and shopping. Then she's up at three A.M. on Christmas morning to put the turkey in the oven and finish the preparations. By three P.M. Christmas day she's in tears, putting a damper on the holiday for everyone.

If your holidays are exhausting, if you can't find half an hour for a bite to eat or a moment's rest, if you're often on the verge of tears, then you're doing too much. It's time to stop and reevaluate.

Force yourself to take time off, sit down and have a cup of soothing herb tea. Go over your "to do" list and eliminate tasks. Be ruthless.

What's the worst thing that would happen if you crossed off half the items on your list? It won't be the end of the world—and it might be the start of a new way of doing things.

Keep reminding yourself that the holidays are not about being in a constant state of panic, fearing you'll never get it all done. They're not about doing so much that there's no time to spend with your kids and your spouse. They're not about feeling you have to do it all and that Christmas won't be perfect unless you do.

I promise, by cutting back you won't lose the spirit, you'll find it.

## Honey, I Shrunk the Holidays

MY FRIENDS BILL AND NANCY both have demanding career schedules, and they have two boys, ages six and nine. In their early years together, Nancy was a stay-at-home mom. She had the time to do Christnmas in a big way, and she loved doing it. But since she returned to work full-time, the holidays are no longer the priority they once were for her. Each year she feels more stressed by the demands of the annual routines she once handled so easily.

Last year Nancy's job required her to spend an inordinate amount of time on the road, so Bill offered to take care of all the holiday preparations. There was only one catch: She had to let him run the show and she couldn't complain—not one single word—when he didn't do things exactly the way she would have done them.

She thought about this. Would Bill spend weeks shopping for gifts for everyone on their list, even picking up extras for unexpected guests? Would he search frantically for just the right wrapping paper and ribbon, then wrap each present, attaching cleverly addressed name tags? Would he polish silver, wash stemware, and prepare the candles? Would he spend an entire weekend before the big day cleaning and vacuuming the house, washing windows and waxing the floors, then rush to the store to stock up on everything needed for Christmas dinner for twelve?

No, Bill probably would not do these things. Most likely he'd be shocked to learn that Nancy did them—as well as dozens of other tasks that women never even have to articulate because they're genetically transferred from one generation to the next.

Let's face it, most guys don't have a clue about these "rules" of getting ready for the holidays. Their wives and mothers have spared them many of the cultural mandates ingrained in every woman's psyche. But even if they knew what was expected, no guy in his right mind would do it all while holding down a full-time job and taking care of two kids.

But Nancy knew that with her travel schedule she wouldn't be able to do Christmas her way. So, as challenging as it was for her, she accepted Bill's offer.

All things considered, they had a wonderful holiday. Nancy had to return only three gifts that Bill purchased, and with tremendous determination she kept her mouth shut when Bill used paper plates for their sit-down take-out pizza dinner. He did remember the candles, though, and by the end of Christmas day, Nancy had stopped cringing about the dust motes on her kitchen floor. She figured her mother-in-law was so shocked by the paper napkins she probably didn't notice anyway.

If you're primarily responsible for the holidays in your household and are now ready to delegate some chores, make up a list of the things you normally do. Then sit down with your family and divide the chores into three categories: what you all agree absolutely must be done, what can be done if time allows, and what can be eliminated entirely. Then divvy up the first and second lists. Determine that you'll maintain a noble silence and stay open to having the holidays be different than the way you've always done them. Come to the realization, as Nancy did, that the only thing that really matters is finding the Christmas spirit, and that you're able to be truly *together* with the people you love.

## *Turn off Madison Avenue*

IT'S NINE P.M. Christmas Eve. You've finished wrapping all the packages and finally have a chance to devour the milk and cookies the kids left out for Santa. You and your partner are busy putting away all the wrapping paraphernalia.

When you're through, you sit together quietly with just the tree lights on, listening to Christmas music playing softly in the background. This is your first chance in weeks to have a quiet moment together. Ah, what bliss.

You take your first real look at the tree. The presents are placed decoratively around it. Michael's new bike is leaning next to the fireplace; Sara's swing is set up in the corner.

But something's not right. Gradually it dawns on you: It doesn't look like *enough*.

You've spent incredible amounts of time—and let's not even think about the money. You bought everything the kids had on their lists and then some. But it just doesn't fit your image of what a wonderful Christmas should look like.

You both look at your watches. It's only nine P.M. You still have an hour before the stores close. You grab your coats and fly out the door, determined to make a last-minute run on the toy department. An hour and a half later you drag in, laden with more packages, wrapping paper, and ribbon. This year you're determined to make it a real Christmas.

By midnight you're finished with everything. Ah. That's better, you think, as you look at the tree and the lights and the incredible number of exquisitely wrapped packages that have taken over the living room. This is how Christmas is *supposed* to look.

We don't have to search far to see where we get these ideas of what Christmas should look like. Advertising, television, magazines, billboards, shop windows, mail-order catalogs, greeting cards, and merchandising displays of every kind artfully turn the season into the stressful, consumer-driven, debt-ridden marathon it has become.

Train yourself to avoid those advertising images. When you can't avoid them, at least recognize the ingenious strategies that are used to lure you into spending money you don't have on things you don't need.

Even if we could afford Madison Avenue's holiday vision, which 98 percent of us cannot, it would still be too much. At the same time, it always feels as if it's never enough. That's the way it's planned. But we don't have to buy—literally—into that contrived version. We can create our own.

## Join the Crowd

YOU MIGHT NOT GUESS it from Madison Avenue's hype, but consumers are already changing the way they do the holidays. According to a *U.S. News & World Report*/Bozell Worldwide Poll, 44 percent of Americans think they spend too much on Christmas. Survey after survey shows that consumers are spending less money on Christmas now than they've spent in the previous eight years. U.S. Commerce Department figures show holiday spending is down by $9.5 billion over the past ten years.

A recent poll conducted by the Center for a New American Dream found that 70 percent of Americans would welcome lower holiday spending and less emphasis on gift giving.

An Associated Press poll conducted in November 1996 showed that 53 percent of Americans expected to earn more money the following year, but 88 percent said they planned to spend less money on Christmas. And they meant what they said. Despite retailers' and economists' wishful predictions that 1997 holiday spending would be up by at least 30 percent, many of the major retail chains reported that sales didn't meet expectations.

These reports leave economists scratching their heads. It used to be such a reliable equation: The more money people have, the more they spend at Christmas. But if these experts looked closer, they might reach the same conclusion many of us have: Spending more doesn't necessarily produce a merry Christmas, and it complicates our lives.

And people are not only spending less, they're spending differently. For example, retail experts report a trend away from toys and material things, and toward gift certificates for camp, spas, college savings, and investments. These are expenditures that focus on personal growth, education, experiences, and the future. Consumers are moving away from costly gadgets that no one needs and that drain the environment and fill our storage spaces.

But keep in mind that because Christmas sales are down, advertisers are more relentless than ever. They'll go to any lengths to entice people back to the malls. They're jumping the season with huge pre-Christmas offerings before

Halloween, and massive radio and television blitzes well before Thanksgiving. They're giving away free parking, valet service, foot massages, and designer coffees to weary shoppers. They're offering so-called bargain prices on everything in the store early in December, rather than waiting until Christmas Eve.

If you haven't already done so, join the move away from holiday spending. In the following chapters, we'll consider some ways to do that.

*Two*

# DISMANTLING
# CHRISTMAS
# PAST

## Let Family and Friends
## Know What You're Doing

IF YOU WANT TO CUT BACK on holiday celebrations and do things differently, let your family and friends know ahead of time so they can make plans and arrange their psyches accordingly.

Decide how you want to do it, then spread the word:

"Okay, kids, last year we spent far too much money on toys you don't even play with, and Daddy and I were so busy we hardly had time to spend with you over the holidays. This Christmas we're going to cut back."

"There were far too many tears and short tempers in our house. Let's talk about how we can have a more meaningful celebration this year."

"I can't face the thought of another Christmas party for as long as I live, so don't even think of inviting me next year." When they invite you anyway, politely decline.

"I love the holidays but they've become far too commercial. I'm not going to get gifts for anyone but the kids next year."

"Honey, Grandma and I have decided that instead of buying you so many toys for Christmas, we want you to come up with something special you'd like to have from us. Then we'll put the rest of the money in a mutual fund for your college education. Do you know what a mutual fund is? Let me explain . . ."

"Hey everyone, we grossly overdid last year, so we're going to spend the holidays in a Tibetan lamasery this year."

Letting people know how and why your holidays will be different makes it easier to change how you do them. It'll also make it easier for others to let go of what they think you should be doing.

· 10 ·

## Take a Poll

IF YOU'RE NOT SURE how your family and friends will react to your decision to simplify Christmas, ask them. You might be surprised at the responses.

Many people are on automatic pilot during the holidays. They just keep doing the same things, whether they like them or not, because they've always done them—or because they believe everyone expects them to. I've talked to many people who say they do all they do for the holidays because they believe their mates, kids, parents, and friends expect it.

In your informal poll of family, friends, and coworkers, some people might be reluctant to answer honestly because they don't want to seem like Scrooge.

Others may have their identity tied up in doing Christmas in a big way, and they're not quite ready to let go of that yet. Still others may be tired of the stress but haven't stopped long enough to figure out why.

Ask sincerely, and you can learn how they'd really like to do the holidays.

You might learn that no one at work wants an office party. Or that many people like the party but would forgo the gift exchange.

You might find that family members are financially strained by having to buy gifts for everyone.

Your spouse or partner might agree to not sending the annual Christmas letter, or agree to do it for you.

You might find that no one would care if there weren't the usual plates of cookies and fudge.

You might find that the very things you dread about Christmas make others feel stressed or overwhelmed, too. Once you bring the question into the open, you've created something that didn't exist before—the possibility of doing it differently next year.

## Be Willing to Compromise

IF YOU TAKE A POLL, be open to changes you don't expect.

Several years ago my friend Henriette sat down with her husband and four kids the first weekend in December. Each family member made a list of five things they liked and five things they didn't like about last year's celebrations. Then they each read their lists aloud to the family.

Henriette was shocked. Not one member of the family liked her plum pudding. Every Christmas for the past sixteen years she dutifully prepared her mother's plum pudding recipe. It took weeks to assemble and was full of hard-to-find ingredients. Each year she made frantic trips to the butcher for the suet. Then she had to find a bank for the shilling, and a specialty store for the miniature airplanes, cars, rings, and other symbolic trinkets that were carefully hidden in the pudding.

She prepared it with such love, remembering all the

while what a treat her mother's plum pudding had been when she was growing up. But her kids can't stand plum pudding. For years they mushed the steaming mound around on their plates pretending to eat it, often not even bothering to look for the lucky shilling that supposedly would bring them wealth, or the miniature airplane that meant travel and adventure in the coming year. And somehow she'd never allowed herself to notice.

Now that the truth was out, however, she realized that even though no one liked it, she didn't want to give up a tradition that was so dear to *her*. So she and the family reached a compromise. She would order the plum pudding from the bakery. When they didn't eat it, she wouldn't feel offended—it wasn't *her* love they were rejecting. And she got plum pudding without having to go through all the trouble of making it.

Mom's plum pudding is now the family's holiday joke, but at least no one has to pretend to eat it.

Another family I heard from found out from their poll that the kids were tired of seeing *The Nutcracker Suite* every year. It was fine the first time or two, but then it got to be old hat. They wanted something different.

Last year, they all went to a neighborhood theater production of *Arsenic and Old Lace*. It was fresh and new to the kids. The tickets were only fifteen dollars instead of fifty dollars, and they didn't have to put on dress-up clothes and drive all the way into the city. With the money they saved, they had a family dinner beforehand at a nearby restaurant.

## · 12 ·

## Gather a Consensus

HOW MUCH HOLIDAY TENSION is brought on by our uncon-
scious need to live up to other people's spending habits?
Once you're on that track, it's difficult to step off—unless
you get everyone around you to agree.

One reader explained how difficult it was for him and his
wife to cut back on holiday spending because everyone they
knew lived so extravagantly. They finally took a close look at
their finances and realized they were playing out of their league.

They had joined a swank health club. The annual fees
were a bit of a stretch but, they thought, manageable. It took
a couple of years to realize that the associations they formed
through the club put them in contact with lifestyles and
activities they truly couldn't afford. Costly sporting gear,
expensive dinner parties, gift exchanges, and holiday trips to
exotic places raised their expenses and created credit-card
debt that was far beyond their means.

Their financial situation became so precarious they were forced to resign from the club. They joined the local Y, where they met people who had less pressured economic lifestyles. This reduced their expenditures and the accompanying stress dramatically.

In getting everyone to agree sometimes it's easier to start with family members—those who love you for who you are, not for what you can afford to give them for Christmas. Sit down with your siblings, their spouses, and parents to see if everyone will cut back not only on gifts, but also on all areas of holiday spending and overdoing.

Then talk with people at the office, your neighbors, and your various social connections. Given that so many of us are tired of the way we've been doing Christmas, it probably won't be too much of a challenge to get friends and associates to do the holidays differently.

When one or more people cut back, it makes it easier for everyone to do so.

## · 13 ·

### Be the First on Your Block

YOU DON'T NEED a consensus to simplify. I spoke to a harried mother in Dallas who moaned, "I want a simpler Christmas, but if I cut back, I'll be the only one I know who does."

Yes! Be the first on your block to have a simple Christmas. If you can't get others to cut back, don't let that stop you from doing things more simply yourself.

If you're not comfortable being a trendsetter, there are many things you can do—lots are detailed in this book—that won't even be noticeable unless you point them out.

Of course it's also possible that other people in your life are as interested as you are in cutting back, but they either don't know where to begin, or they don't want to suggest it first. Chances are great that as friends, family, and neighbors notice that your family is less stressed and having more fun over the holidays, they may ask what's happening. Then you can tell them.

## · 14 ·

## Let Go of What You Think
## Are Other People's Expectations

I SPOKE TO A YOUNG WOMAN in Tacoma who told me about the homemade Christmas tree ornaments she made one year for her family. They were beautiful, delicate creations, and the recipients were thrilled with this unique gift. The ornaments were such a success that she did them again the next year, adding a few more people to her list. By the third year people were asking ahead of time if she would be giving her ornaments again. She was so flattered and pleased that she said yes. Each year the ornaments were more elaborate and more names were added to the gift list.

In time the project took on a life of its own, becoming complicated and extensive. It reached the point where she was planning designs and shopping for materials in January for the following Christmas. Making these gift ornaments had taken over her life, but it never occurred to her that she could simply stop making them. Everyone expected them. How could she disappoint all these people?

It was so stressful that she developed severe carpal tunnel syndrome and had to stop her handiwork altogether.

But a funny thing happened when she told people she wouldn't be making ornaments that year. Nobody seemed to mind. At first she felt hurt. She'd turned ornament making into the focal point of her year, but no one else felt as strongly about it as she did. After she got over her disappointment, she was flooded with a sense of relief.

Often what we think are other people's expectations are ones we conjure up for ourselves. Gift giving, decorating, cooking, wrapping, and holiday activities of every variety easily become competitive sports, but often the only person we're playing against is ourselves. If you no longer find the contest rewarding, quit for a year and see if anyone cares.

## · 15 ·

### Stop Being a Perfectionist

HOLIDAY TRADITIONS provide opportunities for families to come together and express their love and affection for each other. That's certainly the ideal. But family members also use these occasions to hold each other hostage. The motivation may be positive—wanting everything to be perfect on this special day. But sometimes it doesn't feel so benevolent.

A reader from Washington, D.C., described how her mother expected her, her husband, and their three children to get on a plane every Christmas and fly to Florida to spend the holiday with her. The first couple of years were exciting, but then they began to dread the ordeal. They had to pack enough stuff for a week's visit, along with several suitcases of presents, and lug everything to the mobbed airport.

This woman pointed out to her mother that it would be much easier if she made the trip to Washington than for the family of five to go to Florida. Her mother found this idea offensive. She had invested many years in creating a perfect Christmas for the family, right down to the last detail. It was hard for her to imagine Christmas any other way.

Finally the family insisted that Mom try it "just for this Christmas." When they picked her up at the airport they were stunned by how many bags and boxes she had. They could barely fit everything in the car. It turned out Mom had brought her version of Christmas with her, including her own pots and pans, because surely the food wouldn't taste the same otherwise.

Most people wouldn't carry their own cookware across the country, but this story does have a familiar ring to it. If you recognize yourself in this picture, consider what would happen if you took a deep breath and let go of the need to control. You might find that the holidays are wonderful even if they aren't your idea of perfect. You might learn that:

Your sister's walnut stuffing tastes just as good as your chestnut stuffing, and is a whole lot easier.

Your brother and his wife would love to bake the pies this year.

Your kids take great pride in decorating the tree on their own, without your hovering presence.

Other members of your family also have a special knack for gift wrapping.

Christmas dinner tastes just as good on a simple white plate as on your colorful "Santa's Reindeer" holiday china.

No one else would bother to hook up the outside lights, and that would be all right.

You might also find that spontaneity can replace some established traditions. It's quite possible that everyone, including you, will be a lot more relaxed and have a better time. And that's how cherished memories are made.

## 16

## *Analyze the "Merry" Myth*

LAST NOVEMBER certain two-page ads ran repeatedly in national magazines and newspapers. They spoke volumes about the commercially prescribed ways to handle the stress of the season. In one version, on the left a droopy, sad-looking Christmas tree stood above the words *depression saddens*. On the opposite page a sturdy, lush tree stood tall above the words *Prozac can help*.

With the tremendous pressure to create the picture-perfect Christmas and the increase in expectations about gift giving and entertaining, a lot of the fun of the season has been lost. For many people, Christmas is anything but merry.

According to a 1996 *U.S. News & World Report* survey, 75 percent of women and 54 percent of men report feeling stressed out during the holidays.

According to psychologists, the Christmas season triggers feelings of loneliness, regret, nostalgia, and failure in many people.

Alcohol, which flows more freely during the holiday season, is a chemical depressant. It doesn't make people jolly.

Even our general health and well-being can be adversely affected. The Centers for Disease Control say the Christmas season creates more health problems than any other time of year. These include heightening of allergies from tree resin and other greenery in the home, more household fires, and the cumulative effects of overeating and overdrinking. And perhaps because of exhaustion, we're more susceptible to colds and flu.

It's true that Christmas isn't necessarily merry for everyone and many people suffer from clinical depression that's exacerbated by the holidays. But much of the tension is caused by the pressure we put on ourselves. That Prozac ad is a wake-up call. By cutting back and doing it more simply, we can eliminate a lot of the stress, and have a merry Christmas without resorting to antidepressants.

## 17

## Close the Family Inn

FOR MANY PEOPLE, Christmas is a time when family and friends from distant places move in and take over the house.

Your adult children arrive on your doorstep with spouses and babies in tow. Old friends who've always wanted to see New York or Los Angeles or Seattle or Duluth drop in for two weeks and appoint you tour guide. Second cousins twice removed decide to renew old acquaintances, and your college roommate, who's been out of touch for decades, is just passing through and needs a place to stay.

With holiday guests your home can be quickly turned into a cross between a bed-and-breakfast and Grand Central Station.

It's wonderful to see loved ones who live far away, or renew old friendships. But when people move in for the duration, it can turn the happiest of occasions into difficult times. It's hard to relax and enjoy guests when you're busy keeping hot meals on the table and fresh towels and linens in stock. The holidays are stressful enough without having to be "on" twenty-four hours a day.

If you're tired of the holiday free-for-all, one approach would be to announce well in advance that you're simplifying the holidays and the inn will be closed this year. Provide a list of inexpensive nearby hotels or motels for those who want to visit.

If there are certain guests you must accommodate, at the very least ask them to pitch in and help with meal preparation, laundry, and cleanup. Post a chores list on the fridge and don't be shy about assigning tasks to guests.

Or ask another family member to be host. Or close the inn, and use the holiday break to get away yourself.

## 18

## Rise Above the Guilt

ONE OF THE BIGGEST challenges many people have in simplifying Christmas is guilt. They feel guilty about not doing enough; they feel guilty about not doing it right. But most often they feel guilty about family.

A reader from Boston told me she dreads the holidays and would love to pass them up entirely. If she had her choice she'd spend them on a white sandy beach somewhere warm, doing nothing. But her guilt at "abandoning" the other members of her family would never allow her to miss their annual celebrations.

A couple from Portland said they'd love to stop having Christmas dinner at his parents' home because there's so much bickering among the relatives. But they don't want to cause any hard feelings. So year after year they make the trek to Grandma's to spend a nerve-wracking, unpleasant day.

But many people have reached a point where they refuse

to subject their families to holiday experiences that lack the love and togetherness they should have.

My friend Paul decided several years ago not to attend his very traditional family's Christmas dinner. He didn't enjoy the tension, the stress, or the annual competition for the most elaborate gift.

He loves his family, and he had put up with extravagant holiday rituals because he convinced himself it was only one day out of the year, so what the heck. But he began to realize that even before Thanksgiving he started to feel uneasy about Christmas. In fact, he had qualms about it throughout the year, and that anticipatory dread soured every other aspect of the holidays for him. He'd tried to suggest ways the family might do things differently, but they were sticking to their traditions.

After much deliberation he gathered his courage and announced that he wouldn't be joining the family on Christmas, and that he was opting out of the gift exchange. He held firm in the face of pleading, cajoling, and wheedling from parents, siblings, cousins, and other relatives. They called him a Grinch. They muttered "bah, humbug" in his presence.

The first year was the hardest. But by mid-January every family member but one had let go of any concerns they had about his absence.

By the second year, the entire family had accepted his decision. Some didn't understand it; they affectionately called him Scrooge but peaceably allowed him to celebrate in his own way.

If your family holiday gatherings damage your spirit, don't let guilt keep you from having the Christmas you want. Let's face it, not every family fits the Norman Rockwell image of the happy group around the Christmas dinner table. If you're unable at this point to deal creatively with dreaded relatives (#89), then maybe it's time to consider other options.

Keep guilt in perspective. On a misery scale of 1 to 10, guilt might be a 4; getting through an excruciating couple of days or even a meal among people you don't want to be with could be a 15. Feeling guilty might be preferable.

Remember, the first year will most likely be the hardest. After that the delight of celebrating a simpler, happier Christmas will quickly minimize the guilt other family members try to lay on you. Then you'll simply rise above it.

*Three*

# CREATING
# A NEW
# APPROACH

❄

## Consider the Origins
## of Your Traditions

IN TAKING A SIMPLER APPROACH to holiday celebrations, it helps to understand how some of our customs originated. Why do we decorate trees and send cards at Christmas? Why do we give gifts and have huge dinners?

Our American Christmas is a mix of pagan practices, religious observances, and cultural traditions. For example, the Christmas tree derives from ancient times when the evergreen was believed to have magical properties because it stayed green during the winter. The tree was a sign of life. Some cultures decorated evergreen trees with edibles like cookies, nuts, and fruits. When the tree was taken down they feasted off its branches.

In the old Roman calendar, December 25 was the shortest day of the year. It was the beginning of the solstice—the renewal of light as the days began to grow longer. Christians later chose this date to celebrate the birth of Jesus, because his birth was a renewal of light for humanity.

The Roman ritual of Saturnalia took place at this time of year because in southern Europe it was the season of the harvest. Saturn was the Roman god of agriculture, and there were great banquets to give thanks for the yield. Our holiday traditions of singing, dancing, ringing bells, and hosting feasts all have their roots in the celebration of the harvest.

Gift giving grew out of the Saturnalia observances as well, and the original gifts were almost always food. Christians continued the gift-giving tradition, teaching that it was a symbol of the ultimate gift of life given through Christ's birth.

Blessings of the season, and wishes for peace and prosperity evolved into the tradition of sending Christmas cards. With the invention of the penny post and the printing press, cards became an affordable way to send good wishes in Victorian England.

The history of our modern celebrations is rich, diverse, and ever evolving. Today people of many faiths and varying backgrounds participate in these traditions. Yet we sometimes get so attached to the external symbols that we lose sight of their deeper meanings. Like all symbols, they can be changed, updated, and re-created.

We don't need to cut down trees; there is an infinite number of other ways to celebrate life. We don't need to have huge meals where everyone overeats in order to give thanks for our abundance. We don't have to go into debt to purchase material objects that add no meaning to our lives.

We can create an entirely new approach that will make the celebration of Christmas what we want it to be for our times.

## · 20 ·

## *Examine Your Current Traditions*

SOMETIMES people worry that if they don't do Christmas as usual, the holiday will lose its magic. In this country, however, many of our traditions are not that old, and the magic is what we bring to them. A lot of the embellishments that are part of the American celebration—like Bing Crosby singing "White Christmas"—are no older than the 1950s.

Many traditions we hold most dear express commercial motivations rather than tidings of good will. Our present-day image of the jolly Santa, for example, expanded from Clement C. Moore's "The Night Before Christmas" into an advertising campaign for Coca-Cola. Rudolph the Red-Nosed Reindeer was originally a department-store gimmick.

The custom of sending Christmas cards became very popular after World War II, when the post office recognized the opportunity to boost stamp sales. Then Hallmark got into the act, and now we have an expensive, time-consuming, environmentally wasteful "tradition" that generates guilt in the heart of anyone who considers discontinuing it.

Keep in mind that America is a nation of both change and tradition. In this century alone, fresh waves of immigrants have infused our culture with different observances and perspectives. With the exception of our custom of consumerism, we would be hard pressed to identify a uniquely American holiday tradition that isn't inspired by bits and pieces of celebrations from other cultures.

It's time to reexamine the way we do things. As we move away from many of our commercially generated practices, we may discover that the only true and enduring traditions are those that add meaning to our family, our community, and our spiritual lives. Then we can arrange holiday observances that express that meaning.

## · 21 ·

### *Explore Other Traditions*

IF YOUR FAMILY decides to restore meaning to the holidays, you might begin by taking a cultural journey. Choose another part of the world and study its Christmas traditions. You could even select a different tradition each year for your own celebration.

You'll learn that no other culture starts the Christmas holidays in September. You won't hear slogans like "Only twelve shopping days until Christmas" in Scotland. You won't find thirty-plus women's magazines describing how to do Christmas in Italy, France, or Germany. Shopping areas in the Middle East don't assault the ears with Muzak versions of "Santa Claus Is Coming to Town" or "Jingle Bell Rock." Santa's sleigh, overflowing with toys, doesn't make stops in most parts of the world.

In many cultures the main focus of the Christmas celebrations is on religious themes and simple practices.

In Italy a piece called a *ceppo* replaces the tree. It's made of wood and looks something like a ladder with shelves. On the bottom shelf is a nativity scene. The other shelves hold decorations and small gifts.

In Spain, Christmas Eve is a purely religious celebration. Families gather before their crèches to sing hymns and pray before going to midnight Mass.

In France, many people pot their Christmas trees so they can be replanted later, a sign of the restoration of life in every season.

In Ireland, there are few Christmas decorations, except for lit candles set in windows on Christmas Eve to light the Holy Family's way.

It's customary in Finland to sprinkle straw on the dinner table in memory of the humble circumstances of the first Christmas.

In Poland, the letters C, M, and B representing the Three Wise Men—Casper, Melchior, and Balthazar—are painted on the doors of homes to insure a good year to come.

We don't have to limit ourselves to our own holiday traditions. We can expand our vistas beyond America to find interesting traditions from other cultures that can help us celebrate Christmas more simply.

## 22

## *Simplify an Old Tradition*

Dear Elaine,

I've always loved the lights and music of Christmas. For years my husband and I made the trek into New York City to see the lighting of the Christmas tree at Rockefeller Center and listen to the carolers.

But it's reached a point where bundling the kids into the car and fighting traffic and crowds for four hours has gotten to be too much, especially with all the other stresses of the holidays. So this year we decided not to make the trip.

Even though I was happy with our decision, part of me missed the lights and Christmas music. As it turned out, we were sitting around the dinner table one night just before Christmas when we heard carolers in the next block. Just for fun we put on our coats and hats and went out to see if we could find them.

We walked one block, then another, then another. Finally we saw other people out, as we were, heading toward the sound of music. Some had steaming mugs of coffee or hot chocolate—they'd obviously done this before.

In the next block we found it. The members of a neighborhood church choir stood on the steps of the church, accompanied by a small electronic organ, singing their hearts out.

Dozens of people from the neighborhood gathered on the front lawn of the church with kids and dogs. Someone from the congregation handed out sheet music and lighted candles braced with tin foil so we could read the lyrics and sing along.

We sang all the carols, but no one wanted to leave, so we started over. We stood there for more than an hour singing every Christmas song we could think of. When we couldn't sing another word, the pastor gave a brief holiday blessing of the crèche. Then we all wandered back to our homes, exchanging heartfelt holiday greetings with friends and strangers, and softly humming our favorite Christmas melodies.

I found out later that the choir does this every year, and I was struck by how much we had complicated our tradition of listening to Christmas music while this simple holiday celebration was going on right in our own backyard.

Yes, it was fun to do the big holiday musical event for a while, and I'm sure we'll think back fondly on those times. But almost by accident we discovered that we could modify our holiday tradition and have a new experience that's just as wonderful as the old one—and a whole lot simpler.

*Cynthia Wright*
Danbury, Connecticut

## 23

## Celebrate Christmas for the Kids

SO MANY OF US say we keep doing Christmas for the kids' sake. Think about how much simpler the holidays could be if we did them *only* for the kids—the ones who are still young enough to believe in Santa Claus.

Kids have no expectations but the ones you establish for them. Just imagine:

You wouldn't spend agonizing hours shopping for the perfect present for dozens of people on your list—just sneak a peek at your kids' letters to Santa.

You wouldn't spend weeks planning, shopping for, and preparing elaborate meals. The grandparents and other relatives could join you for a simple meal and a gift opening for the kids, knowing there wouldn't be a big production.

No outrageous decorations are necessary for those little people who don't really care how the halls are decked. A simple tree trimmed by the family would do the trick.

You could eliminate all the other Christmas parties—and the fattening pâtés, delicate breads, and fancy desserts.

Without all the parties, no one would need expensive new outfits.

What child expects you to send Christmas cards?

What child needs elaborately wrapped packages? Use last year's wrapping paper, and you don't even have to iron it. Or forget wrapping altogether; our ancestors didn't wrap presents—do we really need to?

Enlist the help of your older kids to keep excitement and anticipation alive for younger siblings, cousins, and friends. This could become part of the fun—telling Christmas stories, sharing their own tales.

You could start Christmas as late as December 22 or 23 and still get everything done without stress. The holidays wouldn't take four months out of the year.

You might have to make a special effort not to compete with other parents, as we do for our kids' birthday parties, but this is possible.

And if you're a kid at heart, get into the mode of creating memorable holiday experiences for the real kids, and have some fun in the process.

If you don't have kids of your own, find some who could use extra spirit—hospitals and shelters are full of them. You've got too much stuff already, and you probably don't need to gain another ten pounds.

## · 24 ·

### *Celebrate Christmas for Mother Earth*

As we've seen, many of our holiday traditions were once associated with the winter solstice, a time of year when ancient people revered the earth as a source of life and nourishment. So what better way to celebrate the Christmas holidays than by acknowledging the seasonal changes, honoring the earth, and protecting the environment?

Involve the entire family. You can have fun and at the same time teach your children a lesson they'll carry with them all their lives. Here are some ideas:

1. The day that marked the beginning of ancient winter solstice celebrations was the shortest day of the year; in our calendar it's either December 21 or 22. After this, the days start getting longer until summer solstice in June. During Christmas week, watch the sunrise and sunset each day. Have your kids keep a chart

of the times, and become sensitive to the change in light as days quickly get longer. Doing this will connect you to the earth as few other things can.

2. In the weeks before Christmas, spend time each day appreciating nature. Go for a walk, or take a hike in the woods or mountains, and be sure to be completely attuned to the environment around you.

3. Choose a piece of earth and commit yourself to taking care of it. For example, clean up a vacant lot. Collect and recycle all the plastic debris on a stretch of beach or around a favorite pond.

4. Use only recycled goods for cards, wrapping paper, and other items you use during the Christmas season.

5. Don't use your car for a week.

6. Decide that you won't release pollutants into the air. Don't use your fireplace or set a bonfire.

7. Make a contribution to your local parks department for the cleanup and maintenance of a neglected area in your community. Ask your friends and relatives to contribute, too.

8. Reevaluate your family's recycling program. Contact your community environmental resource group

and find out if they have changed their recycling policies to include more items. If you don't recycle, take time to find out how to get started.

9. Adopt an endangered species. Decide together as a family what animal you'd like to help save, then gather information about that species. Write letters of protest or make phone calls to companies that are harming them. Denounce the abuse to local or national government agencies. Make informative posters and put them on public bulletin boards, or join an organization that's dedicated to rescuing that species.

10. Eat only natural, organic, or unprocessed foods for a week. The entire family can help plan and prepare a Christmas meal that's healthy and easy on the environment.

While you're celebrating your environmentally friendly Christmas, set aside a special time during the week to make entries in a family journal and write down your ideas and reflections. Include photos or drawings of your activities. Let each person talk about how it felt to be fully engaged in the preservation of the earth.

## 25

## *Become a Kris Kringle*

Dear Elaine,

I want to share with you one of the traditions that has made the holidays special for our family. For years we have participated in our church-sponsored Kris Kringle program. You don't have to do it through a church; any group of people—schools, corporations, or any organization—can get together and do this.

Each year we get a list of names of people in our parish, such as a family who is struggling financially, an elderly shut-in, a sick child, or anyone who could use some help. In almost any community you can contact a church or service agency for a list of needy people.

We put the names in a basket and each Kris Kringle participant draws one. Then, anonymously, we do special things for them in the weeks before Christmas.

We always start on the first Sunday in Advent and continue several times a week throughout the month of December until Christmas Day, putting together special surprises for the name we've drawn.

Our kids find it so exciting to participate in this project. They take it seriously and think carefully about what we could do for our Kris Kringle people. If there are children in the family, we find out their names and ages and leave them special child-oriented treats and gifts. We never spend a lot of money or buy expensive gifts. We make tree decorations for them and give them clothes and toys we know they could use.

Whenever we prepare a casserole or bake bread or cookies, we make some extra for our "Kris Kringle family." We might buy a small tree, or put together a basket of food, or a box of toys with a note signed "K.K." and leave it at their front door.

I think we often get more out of it than the recipients. It's so rewarding to do something thoughtful for people who need help, especially when they don't even know who's doing it.

Perhaps you might like to tell your readers about this idea.

*Martha Roberts*
Annapolis, Maryland

## 26

## Have a Silent Night

WHEN I WAS GROWING UP, my school scheduled a week of silent spiritual reflection each spring and fall. Instead of attending our regular classes, we listened to lectures, participated in prayer groups, and had extended times of quiet contemplation. Even the youngest students were expected to maintain silence—both at school and at home—throughout the week.

Our parents were encouraged to observe silence during the evenings as well—with no TV or radio or other distractions—to set an example and encourage this time of prayer and commemoration of the spiritual in our lives.

This was always a rewarding experience for me, and it instilled a deep understanding of how one could celebrate in silence.

In recent years I reinstituted silence as part of my spiritual practice. I now spend one day a week in silence. Gibbs and I have our meals and walks together in that silence. It provides the opportunity to communicate with each other at new and deeper levels.

With all the hubbub that surrounds the holidays, having a period of silence is a wonderful gift to share with your children and other loved ones. Start with a silent evening. Or spend even an hour of reverential silence on Christmas Eve. That silence will connect you with others in ways that are far more potent than speech.

"Silent Night" is a favorite Christmas carol for many of us. Just think of the *feelings* those words—*silent night, holy night, all is calm, all is bright*—invoke in your heart. With a little practice, having a true silent night could become one of your favorite traditions.

· *27* ·

## *Have a Holiday Retreat*

IF YOU'RE USED to waking up the day after Christmas feeling overstuffed, overspent, exhausted, and let down, imagine what it would be like to wake up feeling healthy, balanced, recharged, and invigorated.

You can make a dramatic change in the way you celebrate the holidays by arranging a Christmas retreat. Rather than using the standard props of decorated trees, presents, and food to inspire togetherness, find it through an inner sense of peace and spiritual renewal. This is something you can do with your partner, with your kids, with the entire extended family, with good friends, or by yourself.

You could arrange a soul-nourishing retreat of prayer, religious study, meditation, dance, or quiet reflection. You could arrange a health retreat to begin a new program of exercise and sound eating habits. You could have a retreat for personal empowerment or relationship enhancement.

You could have an environmental retreat to help you get back in touch with nature.

Any destination can be suitable for a retreat. Consider a wilderness cabin, a monastery, a resort, or even a ranch or farm that will give you an opportunity to get in touch with the land. Read *Transformative Adventures Vacations & Retreats* by John Benson (New Millennium Publishing, 1994), and *Vacations That Can Change Your Life* by Ellen Lederman (Sourcebooks, Inc., 1996) for other possibilities.

If you can't get away over the holidays, create a family retreat at home, which will be less expensive and much simpler. Choose a theme—inner growth, health, nature—and plan special activities for the kids.

Taking a family retreat will carry you into the new year feeling emotionally lighter than a so-called traditional Christmas that is no longer fulfilling.

## *Do the Family Arrows*

SOME YEARS AGO friends introduced me to what they described as a Native American tradition: the annual arrows ritual. As it was told to me, each year at winter solstice Indian families of various tribes gathered at sunrise to make a declaration to the Great Spirit. They prepared six specially carved arrows for this occasion. Three represented the things they wanted to eliminate from their lives, such as bad crops or poor health; the remaining three symbolized what they wanted to come into their lives.

They dedicated a holy spot on the ground by spreading dried tobacco leaves in a ten-foot circle, leaving an opening to the north. Then, one by one they entered the circle, stuck their first three arrows into the earth, and publicly made their request to the Great Spirit. When everyone had made their declarations, the arrows were lit and burned to ashes as a symbolic statement representing the eradication of these things from their lives.

Then they moved to "higher ground" with the remaining arrows. Again, they inscribed the circle, this time leaving the opening to the south. When everyone had made their declaration, they stood in silent gratitude to the Great Spirit. They didn't burn these arrows, but left them standing to remind the Great Spirit of their entreaties.

I first did this ceremony over the Chistmas holidays with a group of friends. We fudged a little. We assumed the Great Spirit would understand that none of us was versed in the art of arrow making, and we used new, sharpened No. 2 pencils to represent the arrows. We taped narrow, brightly colored five-inch ribbons to the eraser end to represent feathers. We used colorful dried leaves in place of tobacco.

We drove up into the hills at dawn and performed the ceremony with our adaptations. In the interest of not littering or creating a fire hazard, we buried both sets of arrows. We assumed that if the Great Spirit could grant our requests, She would remember what they were. We've continued this tradition for many years and have never failed to be amazed at the results. Not all of our requests are granted, but some have been granted in breathtaking ways.

The ritual of making the "arrows," tying them with ribbon, listing the things each arrow represents, getting up before dawn, and the rest of these activities sends a powerful message to our subconscious. This opens the way for us and the Great Spirit to bring about those things we want in our lives.

Of course, the power of a request is related not only to the sincerity and intensity of the moment, it also requires follow-through. But new rituals often energize us to follow through in new and effective ways.

The arrows ritual, or your own adaptation of it, is another way to focus on who you are and how you'd like to be rather than on what you give and what you get.

## 29

## Choose to Be Alone

I TALKED with a television talk-show host recently who discovered that she truly loved to be alone over the holidays. For years she's had a hectic professional life, spending much of her time being "on." The holidays are a block of time each year when she can reflect on her life and think about what she's done during the past year, and what she'd like to do in the coming year.

Her biggest problem with this decision was family and friends. Most of them thought it was unnatural to prefer being alone at Christmas. They begged and pleaded with her to change her mind, and in the spirit of sharing and goodwill, offered enticing invitations to various holiday celebrations.

For several years she told people she was spending the holidays with friends just so they wouldn't worry about her, and to make it easier on herself. But she finally realized that in doing this she was denying to herself and to them a part of who she really is: a person who *enjoys* being alone over the holidays.

She decided it was time to let people know that this is a sacred season of the year for her, which she chooses to spend in her own way. She made a special request: "This is who I am. Please accept what I want to do and how I want to spend my time, even if you don't agree with it. Don't feel sorry for me because I want to be alone."

If you choose to have quiet time on your own over the holidays, don't apologize for it, and don't make excuses—it might be unusual, but it's not unnatural. Enjoy it. And realize that a quiet holiday on your own can be a lot more satisfying than the exhausting excesses many people indulge in.

Whatever you do, don't accept invitations because you're afraid people won't understand. Many people won't, but that doesn't mean you have to spend Chirstmas with them.

If you crave that time alone but can't envision changing your Christmas Day gathering with your family right now, be sure to schedule another day during the season for your own renewal.

## 30

## Return Christmas to Its Humble Beginnings

WE'VE COME TO ASSOCIATE Christmas with lavish celebrations, overflowing tables, and a dazzling array of lights, music, and presents. It's ironic that this day is so often celebrated in an orgy of overconsumption, when the first Christmas took place in a humble stable.

What would it mean to create a less extravagant Christmas?

It might mean teaching your kids to enjoy the things they already have, rather than acquiring more in shopping malls.

It might mean being thankful for your health and well-being. Ask yourself what you really need to be happy. Look for someone who doesn't even have that much, and figure out how you can share your good fortune with them.

It might mean finding a way to acknowledge what you have in common with others—even those who seem different from you. If you hold a bias against any individual or group, let go of it for a day and notice how you feel.

It might mean setting up a brainstorming session with people to talk about what you can do to reduce the commercialism and keep the holidays humble and merry.

It might mean making your own contribution to peace on earth. Ask yourself what one individual can do to help further goodwill in the world. This could mean simply listening with an open mind to someone who differs from you. Imagine what would happen if one or ten million others took this step, even for a day.

## 31

## Listen to the Wise Men

THE ACT OF GIVING and receiving is a fundamental part of human interaction. It's our nature to make connections with other human beings and to express our reliance on and love for one another.

I've spoken to many who say the thing they love most about Christmas is giving. But a lot of people are beginning to question the on-demand giving that is a by-product of the commercialization of Christmas. The message of the wise men has gotten lost beneath the piles of neckties, sweaters, perfume, jewelry, toys, and electric shoe polishers that collect under our Christmas trees.

As our Christmases are more and more influenced by commercial interests, they have little to do with love and more to do with accumulating material things, competing, proving ourselves, and trying to meet false expectations. We've lost our way. It is said that the three wise men found their way by following a star. If you're serious about returning to the true spirit of Christmas, perhaps it's time to set your sights beyond the clutter that fills the holiday season and find your own star—the clear beacon that will restore the meaning of giving for you.

People around the country are finding their star by helping others who are less fortunate.

They're serving meals in soup kitchens during the holidays—and all year round.

They're visiting prisons and transition houses whose occupants have perhaps never been exposed to the true spirit of giving.

They're joining Habitat for Humanity (121 Habitat Street, Americus, GA 31709, 912-924-6935) and spending two weeks building housing for the homeless.

They're joining Global Volunteers (375 East Little Canada Road, St. Paul, MN 55117, 800-487-1074) and building schools in Costa Rica.

They're signing up with the Plowshares Institute's traveling seminars (P.O. Box 243, 809 Hopmeadow Street, Simsbury, CT 06070, 860-651-4304), visiting Africa, Asia, Latin America, and Eastern Europe to generate new levels of global understanding and to explore the social, economic, environmental, political, and cultural concerns of other peoples.

They're going on walks with International Peace Walk (4521 Campus Drive, Suite #211, Irvine, CA 92715, 714-856-0200) to promote friendship and diplomacy between ordinary people.

Step out of your comfort zone this year and join them. Find someone in your world, your community, your neighborhood, or even in your own family who could use your help.

Give of your time and yourself and teach your kids this invaluable lesson. If you do, I guarantee you won't wake up the day after Christmas feeling hollow and empty and wondering what the spirit of giving is all about.

· *32* ·

## *Don't Get Wedded to the New Approach*

THERE'S SOMETHING ABOUT THE HOLIDAYS that creates the need to stick to tradition. If you do things differently one year, the expectation is that you'll do Christmas that new way next year. It's so easy to fall into a rut all over again.

Simplifying is a process, so you may not get it exactly the way you want the first year, or even the second. It may take some experimentation to come up with a way of celebrating that's right for you.

There are no rules that say you must keep doing Christmas the same way you've always done it, or that you have to do it the way you did it last year. You can make it up as you go along, taking a new, more meaningful approach from one year to the next.

In fact, you could simplify the holidays by deciding that the only tradition you'll continue is creating a new and happy holiday each and every year.

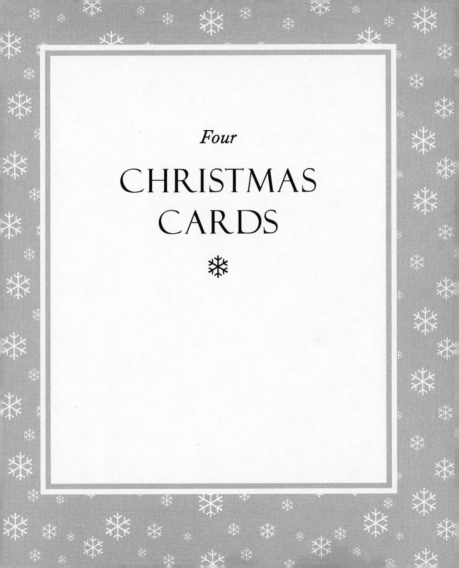

*Four*

# CHRISTMAS
# CARDS

❄

## Rethink Your Christmas Card Tradition

THERE'S NO QUESTION that writing Christmas cards is a source of personal conflict for many people. How often have you heard yourself saying, "If only I didn't have all those cards to address and stamp and get into the mail!"

How much guilt have you experienced over the years because you couldn't write anything more personal than "Merry Christmas"? Sending cards is an opportunity to express warm sentiments and let others know how you're doing. But who has time to write to several hundred people each year?

In my book *Simplify Your Life*, I suggest one way to make life easier is to stop sending Christmas cards altogether. This was addressed to all the people who loudly complain each year about having to do the cards chore. I heard from many people who were overwhelmed by Christmas cards and who liked the idea of discontinuing the practice. But they'd been sending cards for years and couldn't figure out how to *just stop doing it*.

If you're ready to start doing Christmas cards differently, here are some ways to let yourself off the hook gently:

1. Don't send cards to anyone this year and see how you feel about it. If you miss it, start again next year, but with a smaller list (#34). No one will notice for one year.
2. Send cards only in the even years.
3. Send cards to only half your list this year; send the other half next year.
4. Assign the task of sending Christmas cards to a different member of the family each year.
5. Do what my friend Sally did—send a final card to each person on your list, wishing them well and announcing your desire to simplify your holidays by discontinuing the practice of sending Christmas cards. Sally got numerous responses back from people saying they too had decided to cut back, and were glad to know why they wouldn't be getting her card next year. Several said it made it easier for them to cut back, too.

6. Do what another friend of mine does. He collects interesting and colorful postcards from his travels throughout the year, then sends them off over the Christmas holidays with a personal message and an interesting anecdote from his trip.

7. Purchase simple, prestamped postcards from the post office and send them with a holiday greeting.

8. Rather than sending cards to your usual list, sit down with your family and have each person come up with a name or two or half a dozen of the people who have positively influenced your life. Send them a card or note letting them know how much you appreciate their contribution.

9. Consider that each year Americans spend $800 million in stamps to send $4 billion in holiday greeting cards. Not only is that a lot of money, that's a lot of trees. And these numbers don't include the human and fossil fuel energy cost to get them to their destinations. Consider that we've reached a point in time where it's simply no longer personally or ecologically feasible to continue this practice.

10. If you're ready to stop sending cards but are still desperate to make that connection with old friends, there's always E-mail.

11. Look forward to the day when your daughter asks, "Mom, what's a Christmas card? Did you used to send them?"

## 34

## Pare Down Your List

IF YOU FIND yourself caught in the Christmas card loop but aren't ready to call it quits yet, here are some ways to clean up your list:

1. Cross off the names of people you haven't heard from or spoken to in two years.
2. Cross off the dentist, the dry cleaner, the bank teller, the insurance agent, your stockbroker, real estate agent, and other service people to whom you send generic cards.
3. Eliminate old business colleagues and college roommates you never see or talk to.
4. Cross off the next-door neighbors from twenty years ago, and the woman who occupied the hospital bed next to yours when you each had your first child.

5. No need to send cards to anyone who isn't in your current address book.

6. Don't send cards to people you see on a regular basis. Wish them happy holidays in person.

7. Resolve to not add any new names to your list. If people don't get a card from you, they won't expect it, and then you won't feel badly about crossing their name off your list.

8. If you feel guilty about dropping a name from your list, ask yourself if guilt is suffecient reason to send cards. Send that person a silent and heartfelt blessing, and realize they're probably experiencing the same dilemma you are. You had your connection through the years; now it's time to move on.

## 35

## Share the Load

MY FRIEND JAMIE used to send a long Christmas letter, out-
lining to her friends and family the various activities she and
her husband and their kids were involved in during the year.
Some years ago she decided she didn't want to do the letter
anymore, so she assigned the task to her kids. The kids wrote
the letter for a couple of years, then they got tired of doing it.
So they came up with an easier way to stay in touch.

When the first greeting cards arrive at their house, Jamie
puts them in a basket on the dining table. In another basket she
keeps their own cards, a batch of pens, and a roll of stamps.
Each night after dinner, they open that day's cards and pass
them around the table for everyone to read and enjoy. They
take time to think about the card and the person who sent it.

Then they each take one of the cards and send a reply
card with a brief personal message. They address the cards
and put them with the outgoing mail.

This way, cards get completed a little bit at a time and the whole family participates in the process. No one has to print up a Christmas card list or worry about updating it—they simply use the addresses from the cards they receive this year.

## · 36 ·

### *Spread It Out*

YEARS AGO I developed my own simple method of staying in touch with friends.

Since I've never sent Christmas cards, I've always been amazed at how many I receive from other people. Recently I realized that my name stayed on people's lists because I always respond to the cards I receive—but not at Christmas.

I keep the incoming cards in a stack on my desk. Starting in the new year, each week at my leisure I send a couple of hand-written personal notes in response to the holiday greetings I've received.

It may take several months to get through the cards, but I never feel any pressure about it. It's an easy way to keep in touch, without the stress of getting several dozen cards in the mail by December 15.

## Send Tidings of Comfort and Joy

EARLY EACH DECEMBER my friend Holly gathers a stack of small note cards and gift tags, which she keeps in her coat pocket with a pen. She sets herself the delightful task of sending a personal message to at least three people each day throughout the season.

She'll write, "I'm so proud of you," on a Post-it and leave it in her daughter's history book.

She'll write, "Thanks for picking up your clothes," on a note and put it in her seven-year-old son's lunch box.

While she's waiting in line at the bank she'll write, "You look great in blue," and leave the tag with the teller.

She'll write, "You did a great job cleaning my desk," to the cleaning crew in her office.

She once wrote, "Thank you for washing my cup," and left it with her check and money when she'd finished her coffee at a neighborhood restaurant. Several months later, when she had coffee in the same restaurant, she got a note with her order. It said, "You're welcome!"

Another time she wrote, "Thanks for remembering my order," and left it next to her plate for the waitress to find. Months later, when she came in for lunch, the waitress remembered her and showed her the holiday card still posted at her work station.

It seems like such a small thing, but acknowledging someone's being, or presence, or contribution, is a simple way to send a meaningful message during the holidays, or any time.

*Five*

# KIDS AND
# CHRISTMAS

❄

## · 38 ·

## *Cut Back on the Number of Gifts You Give Your Kids*

WHEN MY FRIEND Jake asked his six-year-old, Emma, what she wanted Santa Claus to bring for Christmas, she said she wanted a plastic stroller baby. Jake realized that he and his wife must have blinked just long enough for Emma to see a television commercial advertising this doll with a stroller that morphs into a bed, then into a changing table, then into a high chair, and back to a stroller.

They tried to dissuade her. They offered classic, more cuddly options. A Raggedy Ann doll. A teddy bear, perhaps. Emma would have none of it. She wanted a plastic stroller baby and that was all she wanted.

So they took her at her word. They got the stroller baby and put a few goodies in her stocking. When she opened the package on Christmas morning, she was ecstatic. They could barely pull her away long enough to open her stocking treats, then she was back to her new doll. She even expressed the hope that all the other little girls she knew were as happy with their gift from Santa as she was with hers.

What a lesson. It teaches us that kids don't come into the world expecting to have two dozen beautifully wrapped packages waiting for them under the tree. We train them to expect that by providing it. Then it never seems like enough, so we keep piling on more.

But the problem is not that it's not enough. The problem is that it's too much. By being more selective and giving less, we make each gift more special.

If you've ever watched young kids open their packages, you know how quickly they get bored and overwhelmed. Then nothing interests them. Try cutting back this year, and notice the difference.

## · 39 ·

### *Talk to Your Kids About*
### *Simplifying the Holidays*

IF YOU'VE GOT very young kids, or kids like Emma who don't want scads of toys, you can minimize the mania by limiting the gifts right from the start. But if your kids are older and used to having lots of packages to open on Christmas morning, sit down with them now and talk about how and why you want to do Christmas differently this year.

There are any number of explanations you can give them: Christmas gift giving is too expensive; shopping is too time consuming; too many gifts adds to the clutter in our homes and our lives; it adds to the garbage in our land-fills; many of the products we consume are a waste of precious natural resources.

You could explain that there are better things to do with money spent on gifts—from taking a special family trip to sharing with a family in need.

You could explain that Christmas is too commercial and you want to recapture the true meaning of the holidays. Ask for their help in deciding how do this. Together you can come up with new ways to celebrate that don't involve going out to buy something.

Don't assume your kids won't be receptive to the idea of cutting back. Most kids are reasonable and can adapt to new guidelines, especially if we make it clear ahead of time what the new rules are, and enlist their help and ideas in the process. Make it a fun and exciting challenge.

One single mom from Seattle told me she was forced by circumstances to teach her two kids to have a simpler perspective on the holidays. They've both thanked her repeatedly for teaching them not to overdo it. They're teenagers now, and they see many of their friends' holiday excesses as frivolous and even silly.

Many parents now realize that less is more. With the proper approach, we can teach our kids that too.

## 40

## *Turn off the TV December 1*

THINK OF TELEVISION as your adversary in the plan to introduce your children to a simpler, more meaningful Christmas. Establish a no-TV policy beginning December 1, or even earlier.

It's television that teaches kids they must have a Sleep n' Snore Ernie, or that all their friends will be getting Power Rangers or life-sized Barbies. Rather than letting them zone out in front of the television, soaking up commercial messages of the season, engage your kids in activities that reflect the real spirit of the holidays.

Talk to them early and often about why watching television is not an activity you want them to engage in. Explain how relentless advertising programs get us to want things we don't need and can't afford.

Read classic Christmas stories out loud. "The Little Match Girl," by Hans Christian Andersen; *A Christmas Carol*, by

Charles Dickens; *The Crowded Inn*, by John McGaw Foster; "The Elves and the Shoemaker," by the Brothers Grimm, and "The Gift of the Magi," by O. Henry. These are just a few of many you'll find in the public library.

Bake cookies together, some to keep and some to give away.

Rent videos of your favorite Christmas movies and curl up on the couch together with the cookies, or popcorn.

Sing Christmas carols.

Spend time in the fresh air hiking, sledding, skating, stargazing, bird watching, or building snowmen.

Take evening walks or drives through the neighborhood to look at Christmas lights.

If you don't want to give up the TV completely, watch only when there's a program that reflects your values and teaches a positive lesson about the meaning of Christmas.

There are a number of perennial TV favorites that relate positive messages. They include *It's a Wonderful Life*, *How the Grinch Stole Christmas*, *A Charlie Brown Christmas*, *Amahl and the Night Visitors*, *Miracle on 34th Street*, *A Christmas Carol*, and *The Nutcracker*.

Watch selected programs with your kids, and teach them how to use the remote control to skip commercials.

## 41

## Say No to Elmo

RECENTLY THERE WAS national hysteria over a toy called Tickle Me Elmo. Elmo is a furry doll that giggles when you push a button on its tummy. It was reported, no doubt by its manufacturers, to be the toy every child wanted and every parent was desperate to purchase.

Newspapers carried stories about fights in department stores, and long lines of hopeful purchasers stretching for blocks. One woman was reportedly held at gunpoint by another parent intent on robbing her of the doll. One man claimed he advertised that he'd sell his Elmo for four hundred dollars, and had hundreds of calls.

One mother, embarrassed about standing in line for three hours to buy Elmo for her daughter, told me, "I know it's terrible, but all the other parents are buying this doll for their kids. If I don't get one, my daughter will be the only one who doesn't have it. What can I do?"

The answer for all parents caught in this dilemma is obvious: Come to your senses. Is this the Christmas message we want to give our children? Is it really worth risking life, limb, and wallet to buy your child a toy that's in demand only because an incredibly expensive and disingenuous ad campaign has made it so?

It's time people took a stand against such blatant tactics. We can count on the fact that every year there will be a new toy that "every child has to have." With loving instruction, even young children can understand that they don't have to have something just because everyone else does.

Learning at an early age not to get sucked into the mindless consumer mentality will be a true gift—and one your kids can use all their lives.

## · 42 ·

## *Zap the Toy Registry*

THE GIFT REGISTRY at one of the major toy stores is a new system that allows children to walk around the store with scanner wands and zap the bar codes of items they want. The selected items then appear on a list available to Dad, Mom, Grandpa, Grandma, and all the aunts and uncles. No muss, no fuss. No disappointment or tears. Your kids can have a perfect Christmas.

If you want your children to learn that the true meaning of Christmas is found in bigger, better, more expensive presents, sign them up for the gift registry, which will no doubt soon be available at all toy stores. It's a sure way to help your kids become rabid consumers before they even reach the age of reason.

No doubt the marketing team that devised this concept has received high praise. After all, their job is to sell as much merchandise as possible. Our job as parents is simply to refuse to go along with such nonsense.

## · 43 ·

### *Teach a Lesson of Value*

A SINGLE MOTHER of two in Dallas told me she had no choice but to simplify Christmas. She just didn't have the money to do otherwise. "When my kids beg for the latest toy, I just tell them that we can't afford it," she said.

I asked if she would buy her kids everything they wanted if she could afford to. This question gave her pause. She admitted that money wasn't the only reason she didn't give her kids lots of expensive stuff at Christmas. It had to do with her values, too. She wanted her children to learn that Christmas wasn't about how many presents they have under the tree.

But she realized that she often used the excuse of not having money when her children asked her for things. The money excuse is an easy way out.

Many parents miss the opportunity to give their children a lesson about values because it's easier to cry poor and leave it at that. This Christmas, when you tell your children why they won't be getting the toy-of-the-moment, offer an explanation that reflects a positive value, and reinforce your family values early, clearly, and as often as you need to. When your kids beg for more, don't make excuses. Tell them, "In our family we celebrate Christmas in a simpler way. We believe Christmas means something more important than getting presents, or getting the same thing everyone else is getting."

Of course, if you really can't afford it, don't be afraid to tell your kids that. It's a positive lesson for your kids to see that you refuse to go into debt for things you can't afford at the moment.

Stress generosity toward those in need as a model for your family. Make your home a place where everyone is considerate of others, not just selfishly concerned with his or her own wants and needs.

When you read the Christmas story to your children, ask them to tell you in their own words what it means to them. Have them help you figure out a way to express that meaning in your family celebration.

Place the emphasis on holiday activities done together to

celebrate the season, instead of the material things you give and receive.

You can expect some resistance from your kids at first. After all, they have the combined pressure of media and peers to contend with. But remember that children still receive their most lasting values from parents. It's within your power to make a positive impact on a new generation.

## · 44 ·

## Give Your Kids the Gift of Time

THE MOST MEANINGFUL GIFTS aren't always wrapped in shiny packages with big bows. Parents often assume their kids will feel deprived if there aren't lots of presents under the tree. But what kids truly love is your undivided attention on a regular schedule they can count on.

Many parents now recognize that time together is the most important thing they can give their kids. As we've already seen, Christmas sales have declined in recent years, while travel over the holidays has dramatically increased. From ski trips to hiking vacations to a week on the beach, families are spending their money creating meaningful experiences together, rather than on gifts that are soon forgotten and end up in the garage or the attic.

This Christmas give the gift of time. It doesn't have to be an expensive trip. One father gave his son a gift certificate promising to play hooky on the first snow day so they could build snowmen together. Another presented his daughter with a kite and the message, "Let's go fly a kite. Pick a day." Here are some other ideas.

Give your kids a subscription to the "Adventure of the Month Club." Plan twelve simple adventures they'll enjoy—a picnic at their favorite park, a trip to the zoo—and make them a secret until the day of the event. You can keep your kids in a state of excitement and anticipation twelve months of the year.

Agree to spend half an hour each day for a year doing whatever your child wants to do. Kids love it when their parents play with them, even though their choice of activities—Barbie tea parties and two dozen hands of Old Maid—can be boring for adults. So to make it a truly special time, train yourself to avoid sneaking peaks at the clock, and enjoy the pleasure of being with your child.

Plan a mystery outing to a favorite spot—a nearby pond to feed the ducks or the park with the best jungle gym. On Christmas Day give your kids a set of clues and instructions that keep them guessing. Make it a game for them to try to figure out the mystery.

Give a gift certificate for a night on the town—dinner and a movie—for just you and the child. If you have more than one child, give each one a certificate for a different night. My cousins Karin and Jim have done this with their four kids for years. Their oldest daughter, who is now in college, makes a trip home each year just to have that special dinner treat with her folks.

Give gifts that are designed to involve the entire family—puzzles, board games, sleds, ice skates, Frisbees, or croquet, badminton, or backgammon sets.

The time may soon come when your kids think they're too old to spend time with their parents. Get them in the habit of spending time with you now, while they're still interested.

## 45

## Give Less, Play More

THE DAY AFTER CHRISTMAS last year Gibbs and I took a walk to a nearby community rose garden, as we do nearly every day to watch the sunset. When we arrived, there were two young couples, obviously related, playing with their five kids, who ranged in age from about eighteen months to six years. An older couple, presumably the grandparents, sat on a nearby park bench cheering them on.

We watched for over an hour as the parents played with their kids. They had no Frisbee, no baseball, no glove, no wagons, no tricycles, no kites, no boomerangs. They had not a single toy or piece of play equipment. They had nothing but themselves.

They played Let's Catch Daddy and Daddy Can't Catch Me. They played Let's Catch Mommy. They played Ring Around the Rosey, All Fall Down. They played Hide-and-Seek and Let's Hide Behind Grandma. They played Toss the Baby in the Air and Daddy Toss Me in the Air. They played Tag and Follow-the-Leader. They played Let's All Roll Down the Hill. They played Let's All Hug and Kiss the Baby. They played Now It's Time to Get into the Car and Go Home. And then they all did.

Gibbs and I were transfixed the entire time as parents, grandparents, and kids laughed, squealed, screeched, and ran around with total abandon, having such fun together.

It was a moving example of how little we need—and how little our kids need—to have a good time.

## 46

## Teach Your Kids to Give

MANY PARENTS COMPLAIN that today's children are too materialistic and self-centered. This is seldom more apparent than at Christmas, when a child's whole focus is on what Santa's going to bring. While it's true that television and our enhanced consumer culture has given kids more materialistic notions of what Christmas is about, children today are probably not all that different from kids of previous generations.

Psychologists and child development experts tell us that young children are naturally self-centered. It's part of the process of developing their identity and feeling safe in the world. A child doesn't automatically understand what it means to care about others or put another person's needs ahead of his own. Nor does a child grasp the effect his actions may have on someone else. These things must be taught.

Here are some ways you can do that:

1. Let your children see you doing things for others, or considering another person's feelings. The best way to teach is by your own example.

2. Make your home a place where generosity is stressed all year long, not just during the holidays.

3. Help your children discover through experience how good it can feel to put another person's needs first. Teach them to share with siblings, or to let a younger child have the first turn.

4. Read your children Christmas stories that stress the importance of giving.

5. Have family conversations about people in the world, or in your own city, who are suffering or have very little this Christmas. Find a way to symbolize that you care about them—even with a simple ritual of lighting a candle and saying a prayer, or sending silent good wishes for those less fortunate. Ask them what they might do to make a difference.

6. Make it a tradition that each person perform one act of kindness each week during the holidays. Then at your end-of-the-week family dinner, members can share what they did and how they felt.

7. Acknowledge their acts of giving. For example, "It was so thoughtful of you to make that special card for Grandma. I know she'll be thrilled when it comes in the mail."

## 47

## Change the Focus

ONE READER shared the story of how she taught her kids to give when they were young. She and her husband made a radical shift in the way they celebrate the holidays so they could change their kids' focus from "What am I going to get?" to "What can I do for someone else?"

They team up with several other families who have the same objective. In the week before Christmas they put the kids to work making Christmas cards for elderly patients in nursing homes and for kids in hospitals. They organize boxes of small toys and prepare homemade candy to distribute.

Each family has their own quiet dinner on Christmas Eve, followed by a simple gift exchange. Then on Christmas they meet with the other families and spend most of the day visiting hospitals and nursing homes. They hand out their cards and treats, and sing Christmas carols. Sometimes they simply sit with an ailing patient.

Though the kids are always excited about putting together little packages of treats to give away, they quickly figured out that the purpose of the gifts is not so much to give as to make a connection with the person who is receiving it.

For example, last year one of the parents asked the second-grade teacher in a nearby school if she would participate by having her students make drawings and paintings for people in hospitals. Her kids then handed the drawings to patients and the elderly in nursing homes as they went on their Christmas rounds. As they distributed these colorful, imaginative works of art they saw eyes light up. They heard stories of past holidays and traditions from other cultures that added a new meaning to their own. In giving, they were also receiving.

The kids have grown to love this annual holiday practice and are always coming up with new ways to make the holidays more meaningful for people who are ill or who have no one to care for them. One year they performed a funny Christmas skit that they had written and produced. Another year they wrote new, sometimes hilarious lyrics to many of the classic Christmas carols and got smiles and laughs from everyone.

As this reader pointed out, there are so many people alone on Christmas, and there are always children in the hospital over the holidays. She admitted that the kids were often better at talking to children and the elderly than their parents were. Kids know intuitively how to relate honestly to others, and they can easily turn a patient's drab day into an exciting one just by showing up and being themselves.

## 48

## Be Unconventional

IN CONTEMPLATING ways to get your kids to think of others, keep in mind the powerful impact it can have for the rest of their lives. I talked to a group of young mothers recently. One woman told us that when she and her sister were in their teens, their mother announced they weren't going to do the holidays the way they'd always done them. Instead, they would go out into the community and help others.

They spent their Christmas money buying food for the homeless. Mom knew that even though there were several shelters in the city, many people still went hungry over the holidays because they avoided the shelters. So she decided to help those people.

In the weeks before Christmas they made lists and planned and shopped for food. They made hundreds of sandwiches with great care and packed them in brown paper bags with cookies, a piece of fruit, a juice drink, and a small signed Christmas card.

On Christmas Eve and Christmas Day they packed up the car and drove into areas of the community where the homeless congregated, and handed out the lunches. At first, people were reluctant to take the bags. But one did, then another, and they saw that it was safe to accept this gift given from the heart.

As they continued, the girls had the opportunity to look into the eyes of people who had so little. They saw pain, suffering, frustration, paranoia, anger. And they saw gratitude.

They saw firsthand how they could actually do something—and such a little thing—to improve someone's life, even if only for a few brief moments. And they saw that it wasn't just the food that did it—although that helped. Mostly it was that someone had taken the time to care.

When this young woman finished her story, she said it was the most memorable Christmas she'd ever had. Then other members of the group told similar stories.

One woman explained her parents' basic philosophy: They felt they owed it to their kids to be unconventional from time to time. When her Mom or Dad first suggested the idea of working in a soup kitchen or sharing with people less fortunate, she and her brothers responded, "Ah, jeez. That sounds weird. Do we have to? Nobody else is doing that. What will my friends think?"

But as they got into the spirit, the sharing became a transformational experience for all of them. In breaking out of the mold, these parents created holidays that are without exception the most extraordinary of their children's lives.

When you teach your children to give, you not only create a more fulfilling holiday experience for them, you also raise adults who find happiness doing things for others, and who can then teach their kids how to do that, too. It's one of the best gifts you can give to your children and to the world.

## 49

## Start a KIDS WHO CARE Program in Your Neighborhood

I HEARD FROM A READER in Orange County, California, who shared her secret for keeping life simple with her six kids. She started a nonprofit neighborhood organization that provides service opportunities for children ages two through thirteen. It's called KIDS WHO CARE, and it is designed to teach kids to think of others—not just over the holidays, but all year round.

It might seem that starting another organization would complicate rather than simplify one's life, but members of the group feel the benefits to their families far outweigh the small amount of time required to run it. They keep activities to a minimum so that it usually takes little more than an hour each month to organize, and duties are rotated throughout the school year. The major responsibilities are notifying other members of meeting times and necessary materials—this they do by phone tree—and arranging for the contributions to reach the proper destination.

Here's how it works. The dozen members meet once a month, alternating in an open-house format. There's very little preparation required, since they work through existing programs and adhere to the same yearly schedule, which looks like this:

October—Mental Health Awareness Month: Contribute used items for a local mental health thrift store and clothing for the homeless.

November—Fund-raiser for the local rescue mission Thanksgiving Dinner. The kids pool their own money to provide meals for the homeless.

December—Contribute and deliver new toys and canned food to the Salvation Army for a needy child.

January—Contribute used Christmas cards for children's art fund-raiser.

February—Make valentines for nursing home residents.

March—Earth Day Activity: Snip six-pack plastic rings, or plant a tree or bulbs in the neighborhood.

April—Each family contributes items for a diaper bag for a needy infant.

May—Contribute used books to a local home for abused children and/or new books to the local hospital.

The activities are all geared to preschool and elementary school–age children who can't always volunteer at traditional community service sites. Any of these can be adapted to your own locale and the service organizations that are available in your community.

This mother reported that KIDS WHO CARE has simplified their holidays because it has cut back drastically on "the gimmees." The kids are less materialistic since they've had an opportunity to see firsthand that many kids have less than they do.

Also, when kids are involved in service activities with their peers, it becomes a socially acceptable way to spend time and have fun. It helps keep them out of malls and video arcades as they get older because they know there are better uses of their time.

The variety of activities exposes the kids to many possibilities for helping others. The parents have also found that regular, ongoing, monthly events have a much more long-lasting impact on the child than just doing good deeds at Christmas. They inculcate the "helping others" mentality at an early age, so it becomes a habit.

Another benefit that a small, low-maintenance grass-roots organization of this type provides is the opportunity for neighborhood families to become better acquainted. This creates a close-knit support system for busy parents by providing instant baby-sitters in an emergency or car-pool participants to share the driving load.

But even if the *only* benefit you get from starting your own KIDS WHO CARE group is that your kids learn to think of others, that would simplify your holidays and your life.

# · 50 ·

## Simplify Parenting

ONE GRANDFATHER told me how he and his wife handled holiday gift giving for their kids and grandkids. This couple has four children who are all married and have kids of their own. There are seven grandchildren now, and the families are spread all over the country.

Years ago the grandparents stopped spending money on Christmas presents. Because all the grandkids live some distance away, it became a challenge to keep up with their clothes sizes and toy preferences. So they established "Camp Grandma and Grandpa."

Each Christmas they send a card to each of the grandkids, inviting them to spend two weeks with them in the summer. They arrange a time that works for everyone, then send the kids airline tickets for their fun time with Grandma and Grandpa. This gives the grandkids a chance to get away from home and have a new adventure each year, and all the cousins get to know each other. It also gives the parents a break each summer, which is *their* gift from the grandparents.

Of course, this does complicate life for the grandparents—but only for a couple of weeks. Then they get to give the kids back.

## Simplify Grandparenting

"My wife and I would love to simplify Christmas," a father of two young boys told me. "But in our family it's impossible; my mother-in-law is the Grandmother of the Century." He described how each year his in-laws inundated their boys with dozens of expensive, elaborate gifts. He and his wife repeatedly explained that they wanted to cut back on toys the kids get, but the pleas fell on deaf ears.

"We've suggested money for college funds, trips with the grandparents to special places, tickets to movies or sporting events. But they won't do it," he said. "My mother-in-law loves the boxes, the wrapping, and the shopping. She asked my wife how we could deny her this opportunity to do something special for her grandchildren."

This is a tough situation—and one that many young parents face. Unfortunately, there's no easy answer for grandparents who refuse to accept or honor your desire to cut back. If you find yourself in this situation it's important to understand that many people don't know any other way to express love except through material objects.

Often the decision amounts to figuring out what's the best for all concerned. You must decide whether to take a stand and deny your parents something they truly enjoy, and run the risk of creating a rift in the family relationship. If you believe it's crucial, for your children's sake, to confront your parents, and you have the courage, that's one option.

Another might be to enlist your children to ask their grandparents for more practical items, such as a computer, books, or summer camp, rather than toys.

You can also make the decision to cut back on what *you* give your children.

Or you can turn the arrival of gifts from Grandpa and Grandma into a lesson on giving and sharing. Explain to your kids that they don't need so much, especially when there are children who have nothing. Ask them to choose gifts to give away to kids in need. Have your kids write thank-you notes to the grandparents, explaining what they did. ("Thank you for the beautiful doll. Since I already have so many, I decided to give it to a little girl at the homelss shelter who'd never had a doll. It made her very happy, and it made me happy, too. I want to do the same thing next year.")

From the mouths of babes, the message may get through.

· 52 ·

## Simplify the Teacher's Life

NOT LONG AGO I gave a talk to a group of preschool and grade-school teachers. One woman asked me what they could do to simplify the gift exchange with kids. I suggested they establish a policy—and communicate it to the kids and the parents—that the kids simply don't exchange gifts.

The audience spoke up in unison and said, "No, no, no. We're talking about the gifts the kids give the teachers!" They said teachers were overwhelmed with little trinkets—and sometimes big trinkets—that the kids, or rather the parents, feel they have to bring to the teacher.

Oh. Well, my answer is the same. At the beginning of December, print a memo that goes home with each student. Explain that though the gifts are truly appreciated, you've run out of room for them. Therefore, you are requesting that parents not send gifts to the teacher over the holidays, or any other time. At the same time, ask that there be no gift exchanges among the kids.

If all the teachers in a school are in agreement, perhaps this could be established as school policy. Being softies, as most teachers are, the ones I spoke to were concerned about seeming to be hard-hearted. But if you're a parent, put yourself in the teacher's position of having to accept items from two dozen or more students and then figuring out what to do with them.

I realize it can be a challenge to explain to your child why he is the only one not taking a gift to the teacher, but this also presents an opportunity to explain holiday excesses to your kids.

As one teacher suggested, if a parent or child wants to express appreciation to a teacher, they can write a note, or create a poem or a drawing, which can be savored, then easily recycled. It's a safe bet that kind of gift will be much more appreciated by teachers everywhere.

*Six*

# GIFT
# GIVING

❄

## Halt the Runaway Train

FAMILIES HAVE A WAY of expanding over the years as children get married and have kids of their own. A family of five quickly grows, with spouses, kids, and in-laws, to a family of thirty-five. If everyone gives a gift to everyone else, the giving becomes overwhelming. The pressure and expense can be enormous. Christmas Eve often finds family members rushing out to buy last-minute generic gifts for a niece or nephew they barely know.

Families who want to halt the gift-giving mania and restore fun and sanity to the holidays might take a tip from a woman I met in Baltimore. Several years ago her family instituted a Christmas gift exchange that's the high point of their season.

On Christmas Eve all fifteen adults and seven kids gather at her mother's home. Each person brings one wrapped unisex gift purchased for ten dollars or less, and places it under the tree. After a casual buffet dinner, everyone gathers in the living room and the fun begins.

They each draw a numbered playing card to establish the order, then the first person selects a gift and opens it. Each succeeding person can take one of the previously opened gifts or one of the unopened ones that are left. This continues until all the gifts are opened.

Sometimes the evening turns into a riotous melee when the first gift opened is one everyone wants. Or two or three gifts become the coveted prizes, with people bartering back and forth, trading to get a gift that the person with a coveted item might be willing to exchange for it. The permutations are endless, and are all done in the spirit of giving and sharing and having fun.

When the kids were younger, they did their own gift exchange in the same fashion, but with child-oriented presents. Now that they're older, they love joining in the fun with the adults.

Her husband's family has a very different approach. They go overboard on Christmas, with each person buying expensive gifts for every other family member. Her mother-in-law, accustomed to more lavish exchanges, was aghast when she heard about the gift game. "How can you possibly buy *anything* for under ten dollars?" she wondered.

But that's the point. In the gift game, no one is trying to impress anyone or prove anything. The gifts are simply props for family fun and sharing.

## 54

## Write a Personal Letter

Dear Elaine,

I was so excited to hear that you're working on a book about simplifying during the Christmas season. I know I'm not alone when I say that this is the most hectic time in my life, so I welcome your advice on making it a more peaceful holiday.

I wanted to tell you about a tradition my family keeps that makes all our lives easier and, well, happier.

We have a rather large extended family which is, unfortunately, scattered all over the world. Buying gifts for every member would be a complicated process. However, we get together every summer for a beach holiday. We fill a hat with the names of all family members and we each draw one.

Instead of investing in an expensive and perhaps useless gift, we write a letter to the person whose name we've drawn, telling her why we love her, how she's impacted our lives, and what we've learned from her. Since we do the name drawing in the summer, we each have plenty of time to consider the person's role in our lives. This practice has made my whole family much closer, more open, and less chaotic around the holiday season.

We mail the letters a few weeks before Christmas and open them and read them aloud on Christmas morning. This way, we feel connected over the holidays even though we're scattered around the globe.

I hope you find this idea helpful.

*Seanna Beck*
New York City

## 55

## *Write a Family Letter*

I SPOKE TO A READER who suggested another approach to the personal letter exchange. Her family consists of her parents, five sisters, a brother, and all their spouses and kids. Each year they draw names. But rather than drawing individual names, each family draws one of the other family names, then writes a letter to the family.

When it comes time to do the letter, the parents and the kids express what the other family means to them. Then they get together for a holiday meal on Christmas Day and share their letters.

This exchange is not necessarily limited to letters. One year the kids drew pictures of each member of the family whose name they'd drawn and the parents wrote a short story or poem to go with each picture.

Another family put on a funny skit that highlighted the year's achievements of the other family. One family presented a photo montage of snapshots taken over the years.

One year all the kids made a video for the grandparents.

The next year the grandparents responded by producing a cassette tape for the kids, giving interesting tales of the family history.

It takes each family a day or so to put their "gift" together, but they find it's a lot more fun and a lot less stressful than spending time in a crowded mall searching for thirty gifts. There are only two rules to this exchange: The gift has to be of a creative nature, and there's a ten-dollar ceiling on the amount spent.

In the five years they've been doing this, these families have created a treasure trove of memories that will last lifetimes.

## 56

## Rethink Your Christmas Stockings

LIKE SO MANY other Christmas traditions, the custom of hanging stockings had humble beginnings among the poorest of the poor.

One fable says that St. Nicholas felt sorry for a very poor family with three daughters who couldn't marry because there was no money for dowries. In the middle of the night, Nicholas secretly arrived at the house and tossed three bags of gold down the chimney. The bags landed in the girl's stockings, which had been hung out to dry. From this story the practice evolved of filling children's stockings with prized delicacies such as fruit or nuts.

Our current custom of filling a sock with nonsensical gimmicks and throwaways is a far cry from the original.

In stores, "stocking stuffers" are often displayed at the checkout counter to take advantage of impulse purchasers—those shoppers who are desperate for things to fill a stocking or fulfill some other Christmas gift obligation. They include everything from refrigerator magnets, miniature soaps, and palm-sized address books to silly windup toys and bottles of perfume no one would be caught dead using. Mass-marketed "stocking stuffers" are rarely anything that anyone needs or appreciates. And they're not inexpensive; it's easy to spend twenty dollars or more on these meaningless items.

If you enjoy stuffing stockings and want to return to the original custom, fill your stockings with fruit, candy, and small, practical items the recipient would actually find useful. You could include consumable items like toothpaste, toothbrushes, shampoo, moisturizing lotion, a paperback book, or fresh fruit, dried fruit, and nuts.

Better yet, fill stockings with these items, then give them to a needy family.

## 57

## Beware the Catalog Trap

PEOPLE SOMETIMES TELL ME they've simplified their gift shopping by buying through mail-order catalogs. My experiences with this method have been fraught with complications.

How many times have you ordered something through the mail only to receive the wrong color? Or found that the size you meticulously calculated from those size charts was wrong? Or discovered, even though the size was correct, that it still didn't fit right? Then you have to go through the hassle and expense of sending the thing back and starting all over. Or the item you order is out of stock and by the time you get it you've forgotten why you wanted it in the first place.

Several years ago my friend Anne decided to eliminate the most time-consuming, frustrating part of her holidays—going to the malls to shop for gifts. So she arranged to do all her shopping by mail.

In early November, Anne borrowed a few catalogs from

a friend and spent an evening selecting gifts for everyone on her list. She filled out the order forms, called the 800 numbers, and charged everything on her credit card. She paid the extra three or four dollars for each item to be gift wrapped and sent directly to the recipient.

But some time later several of the catalog companies notified her that the items she ordered would not be available for Christmas delivery. She had no choice but to rush to the mall to replace those gifts, and didn't avoid the crowds after all.

But the real shocker was yet to come. Nearly every week for the following year Anne's mailbox was crammed with catalogs—not only from the places she'd ordered gifts from, but from dozens of others as well. Because she hadn't asked them not to, the catalog companies sold her name to other catalog companies. It took her months to get her name removed from those lists.

Even if catalog shopping is simpler for you, be aware of how seductive it is. Those four-color displays are so beguiling that you end up spending more than you planned. Some catalogs play mercilessly on our compulsion to buy, or on our guilt, so it's easy to order more than you need.

Selecting, wrapping, and giving a gift is an intimate act. Catalog gifts are often impersonal. There's nothing particularly intimate about dialing an 800 number to have twenty-five sterling silver key chains factory wrapped and sent to your nearest and dearest. And catalogs can easily encourage the same kind of consumer frenzy one feels in the mall.

Be on guard when the holiday catalogs start arriving.

## · 58 ·

## *Maintain a Twenty-Five-Mile Radius*

I HEARD FROM ONE READER who was so tired of shipping gifts to family members and friends in other parts of the world that she established a new rule: She never buys gifts for people who live outside a twenty-five-mile radius of her home.

Her theory is that she doesn't want to give a gift to someone who can't look her in the eye when they thank her. She figures this way she has a better chance of determining if the gift was appropriate and truly appreciated.

She instituted this practice when she learned that the items she'd been shipping for years to her sister and her niece were frequently not suitable. Her sister appreciated the thought and always thanked her profusely, but never had the nerve to tell her when the gifts didn't work—the style was off, the size was wrong, or whatever. It seemed too much of a hassle to send them back for replacement. It was easier to thank her graciously, then pass the gifts on to someone else or put them in the back of the closet. Finally, her sister got up the nerve to be honest about the presents.

When you think about it, gift giving has truly gotten out of hand if you have to buy, wrap, box, and ship gifts to people you never see anymore, even if you are related to them. They're probably as tired of doing it as you are so it might be easy to get them to agree to stop this by-mail gift exchange. I encourage you to think carefully about this. Ask yourself honestly if there's anything these people really need or want that they can't much more easily acquire for themselves—and get what they truly want. Or are you needlessly complicating your own life and unwittingly adding to the clutter in theirs?

Send cards or make a special holiday phone call to those who live outside of close driving range, and save gifts for people to whom you can hand-deliver them. This makes it easier to determine who's allergic to twelve-grain bread, who can't abide chocolate-covered ants, and who wouldn't wear electric orange even if it is the lastest fashion statement.

## 59

## Avoid the Day-After Blues

IF YOU'RE LIKE MOST PEOPLE, you spend the month before Christmas in a flurry of shopping, cooking, decorating, wrapping, and entertaining. The Big Day has come and gone. So what do you do the day after Christmas? Go to the mall, of course.

Throngs of frantic shoppers line up in malls on December 26 for that universally dreaded post-Christmas ritual: returns. People are absolutely desperate to return:

The polka-dot Polarfleece jacket no one under the age of two would wear, even if it were twenty degrees below zero.

The silk camisole in extra large. (Whatever was he thinking?)

The Happy Face silk tie.

The velour pants and pullover ensemble that only a beached whale would find attactive.

The bright red sweatshirt embossed with the designer's name in large letters.

The coffee mug inscribed "Big Daddy."

The singing bird feeder.

The day-after crowds are grumpy, tired, and short on patience. Not even the most dedicated shopaholic wants to be there. Yet it's estimated that Americans return 116 million holiday gifts each year.

It's possible to give a gift that is truly special and from the heart. Why do we persist in giving gifts nobody wants or needs?

We do it because we live in a culture where everyone we know already has everything they need and a garage full of stuff they don't need. There's nothing left to get someone who has everything but a "Big Daddy" mug or a singing bird feeder, or some other soon-to-be garage-sale reject.

It's time to change our gift-giving pattern. Consider the

possibility that rushing out to buy a mass-marketed, store-bought "gift" is the act of a desperate person. If you doubt this, visit any women's lingerie department on Christmas Eve.

Consider the possibility that putting down a piece of plastic to acquire for someone else the exact same item that millions of other people are acquiring for someone else, and that will probably be returned, is not a particularly creative or original way to express your love.

Consider the possibility that because we've done it for so many years, Christmas gift buying is a habit. It takes very little thought and no ingenuity to just keep doing what we've always done no matter how tired we are of doing it.

You can help your loved ones avoid the day-after blues by making your gifts nonreturnable (#64) or make your gifts consumable (#63). Better yet, find someone who truly needs something (#69).

## 60

## Examine Your Motives

A FRIEND OF MINE told me that what she loves most about
the holidays is giving. She spends hours every year shopping for all the members of her family, selecting just the
right thing for each—though she admitted it was exhausting and expensive. When I suggested that giving baked
goodies or tickets to the theater wouldn't be as tiring, she
said that just wouldn't do. As we talked, it became clear to
both of us that it isn't the giving she loves, it's the shopping.

This is not surprising, considering that shopping has
become America's favorite pastime. On average, we now
spend six hours a week in the mall, and only forty minutes
a week playing with our children. For many, shopping is an
addiction. What better way to feed this habit than by suc-
cumbing to the holiday shopping hysteria that is culturally
sanctioned and expected by our family and friends?

Holiday gift buying is blatantly promoted, and you'd have to look far and wide to find someone who wouldn't be shocked that you were considering *not* buying gifts at Christmas. So it's easy to throw up one hand in mock disgust at having to fight the crowds at the mall, while eagerly starting the engine of your car with the other.

But we don't have to continue this charade. The next time you find yourself in the mall frantically searching for just the right thing for someone on your list, stop and ask yourself why you're *really* shopping. Is it the thrill of buying something—anything? Have you been guilt-tripped into accepting the belief that in order to find true meaning in the holidays you have to *purchase* something? Are you one of those people for whom spectacular gift buying has become a badge of honor?

Take time to figure out if buying something is the only option, or are there other, more appropriate ways to express your love or appreciation to this person. Learn to make the distinction between wanting to give and wanting to shop. Then you can decide if shopping is an activity you choose to continue.

Don't approach cutting back on shopping as deprivation; think of it as liberation. In addition to freeing yourself from consumer debt, you'll be free of the traffic, the noise, the pollution, the crowds, and many of the other things we don't like about the holidays.

## 61

## Take the Affluenza Cure

THE ANTI-AFFLUENZA movement is making appearances in shopping malls around the globe. Its goal is to provide a cure for the buying epidemic that takes hold every year at Christmas.

Affluenza is highly contagious, especially in shopping malls. Its symptoms include the perception that no matter how much stuff you've bought, it isn't enough; the inability to pass a store without going in, even when you've finished your shopping; the annual attack of amnesia about how miserable you were last year trying to pay off your credit card debts; and the absolute conviction that your child *needs* a Beanie Baby to survive in the world.

There is help for this malady. A group in Charlottesville, Virginia, calls itself S.C.R.O.O.G.E., which stands for the Society to Curtail Ridiculous, Outrageous, and Ostentatious Gift Exchanges. Among other things, they encourage people to keep their gift budgets to less than 1 percent of their net annual income. It boasts 2,500 members world-wide. Since 1978 they have published an annual day-after-Thanksgiving newsletter to help people cure their affluenza. You can receive a copy of the newsletter by sending $2 to them at 1447 Westwood Road, Charlottesville, VA 22903.

Several years ago a nonprofit group in Vancouver, British Columbia, instituted Buy Nothing Day, celebrated on the Friday after Thanksgiving. The members hand out checklists to mall shoppers to help them think twice about buying. The questions they suggest you ask yourself—with some of my own thrown in—are designed to help minimize this affliction:

Do I need it?

How many do I already have?

How much will I use it?

How long will it last?

Am I able to clean, repair, and maintain it myself?

Am I willing to?

If not, how much will it cost to have someone else maintain it?

Are the resources that went into it renewable or non-renewable?

What will happen to it when I've lost interest in it?

Will someone else be able to use it?

Will it end up in a landfill?

Is there anything I already own that I could substitute for it?

Can I get along without it?

What's the worst that will happen if I don't buy this now?

Can I wait a month for it? Six months? Even longer?

For the past ten years they have produced a quarterly magazine, *Adbusters*, which has subscribers in over twenty countries. To subscribe, or get information on how to participate in Buy Nothing Day in your area, contact them at Adbusters Media Foundation, 1234 West 7th Avenue, Vancouver, BC V6H 187 Canada, 604-736-9401.

It's encouraging that more and more people are reaching the conclusion that the meaning of Christmas cannot be found in a shopping mall.

## 62

## Ask Family and Friends
## Not to Give You Gifts

*Dear Uncle Bucky and Aunt Mamoo:*

*I want to tell you how much I like the hand-held windup "place it anywhere" massager in the shape of a dodo bird that you gave me for Christmas this year. Those cute orange feet fell off the second time I used it, but it was a real kick while it lasted. And that bird really did walk across my back as the instructions said it would.*

*Jack is still intrigued by the battery-operated seventy-two-tie-capacity Tie Butler you sent him. Now he's thinking maybe he shouldn't have given all his ties away when he got out of the corporate rat race. But he's convinced he'll one day use the "Snuggle Buggles" aromatherapy vibrating foot masseur you gave him—the one that comes from "the Sister Planet TheraPeutic to gobble up all your stress and calm your anxiety."*

*Isn't it fascinating the things they think of for people to give as Christmas gifts? I suppose they've got to keep churning out fantastic stuff to buy or the manufacturers would go out of business.*

*We have a small request, however. I know how much it means to you to search out these clever gifts. And I understand that making a charitable contribution in our name just wouldn't do it for you. But you may remember I mentioned that we've simplifed our lives. The fact is, there really isn't anything we need, though we do always appreciate the thought. We'd be thrilled with a simple phone call from you.*

*In fact, that would make us ecstatic.*

*Your devoted niece,*

## 63

## *Make It Consumable*

WE'RE ALL WIMPS when it comes to telling each other that we don't really want anything for Christmas. But at the very least we could insist on asking for and giving consumables.

Consumable gifts are so practical. Everyone has a favorite taste you can cater to, from chocolates to fruit to cheese to baked goods of every variety. (But this doesn't mean *you* have to bake it if you're not so inclined—get something special from the bakery.)

Edibles are not the only consumables. Soaps, bathing salts, shaving cream, shampoo, cue ball powder, surfboard wax, boot cleaner—the list is endless. Be creative, and have some fun in the process.

The beauty of consumables is that—when thoughtfully selected—they get *consumed*, and therefore don't clutter our homes and our lives. So . . .

*P.S. Uncle Bucky and Aunt Mamoo, if you insist on sending us something, is there any chance you could make it consumable next year? We don't want to seem ungracious, but whatever you do, don't send us one of those shark-shaped cookie jars that plays the theme to* Jaws *when you put your hand in its mouth. Please, just send the cookies.*

## 64

## *Forget the Goods, Give the Services*

IF YOU'VE DECIDED never to spend time shopping in a crowded mall again, there are many nonmaterial, nonreturnable gifts to give the people you love. Here are just a few options:

Tickets to a movie

Dinner out with friends

Dinner in with friends

A day together at a favorite museum

A week of shuttle services

A home-delivered gourmet dinner

A gift certificate for a massage

The services of a professional housekeeper for a day

A certificate for window cleaning

A phone card for out-of-town family or friends

The use of your 800 number for a month

A promise to change the oil or rotate the tires for someone who's not mechanically inclined

A week of pet-sitting for a friend who has travel plans

An evening of baby-sitting for young parents

An evening of parent-sitting for someone who cares for an ailing parent

An afternoon outing for a shut-in

A certificate to mow the lawn, rake the leaves, or shovel snow

Skill sharing: computer advice, letter writing, résumé designing, singing lessons, nutrition evaluation, an aerobics class, or any other special skill

A promise to clean out closets, drawers, and storage spaces, package the memorabilia for family members, then take the rest to the thrift shop

Look around. Be creative. Find a need and fill it.

## *Exchange Your Treasures*

I HAVE THREE FRIENDS who've stopped buying each other gifts for holidays or birthdays. They each have so much that buying things for each other is frivolous.

But they still want to acknowledge their appreciation for each other's presence in their lives. So they draw names and exchange some of the cherished items they each already have. The items can be readable, wearable, smellable, or edible, and include favorite earrings, perfume, scarves, perhaps a sweater, an evening bag, or a batch of homemade fudge. Except for the wearables, the gift has to be small enough to fit in a handbag, so they won't need a truck to get it home.

This idea, or an adaptation of it, is a fun, simple way to give and receive during the holidays without shopping, going into debt, or adding to our landfills.

## *Don't Cave In*

FOR MANY YEARS I got together with a group of friends for a holiday lunch date and our annual gift exchange. After a couple of hilariously mismatched exchanges, we had a cache of items that we had little use for. So one year we agreed that we would stop the gift giving, but continue to get together for lunch.

However, as the holidays approached and we set the date for our lunch, I *knew* some of the others would fudge on our agreement and get "just a little something" for everyone anyway. So I fudged, and got "just a little something" too.

And sure enough, practically everyone had brought along gifts, just in case. No one wrapped the "little somethings," so it would seem more in keeping with our agreement, but a gift by any other name is still a gift, so we were back to square one. And the next year the same thing happened: We all agreed not to bring gifts, but at the last minute some caved in and did.

Finally, someone said, "Okay, this is it. There's nothing any one of us needs. We're going to stick to our agreement, no matter what."

The next year most of us did, and the following year all of us did. We still have lunch over the holidays and we all look forward to that time together, but we've finally reached a point where getting together is what counts. The gifts are just a distraction.

Sometimes it's challenging to change our long-held group or family practices. But if you've all agreed that routines you once engaged in no longer have special meaning, it's time to come up with a new approach and stick to it. If someone renegs, that's their problem, but it's no excuse for you to cave in, too.

## 67

## When Someone You Love Insists

Dear Elaine,

I heard you speak in Columbus recently on how the holidays complicate our lives, and I wanted to share our family's story about how we simplified that hectic time.

I have nine siblings. Growing up we didn't have a lot of money, so by necessity our holidays were pretty simple. We all have fond memories of our Christmases because our folks made an effort to provide little surprise treats for each of us that we eagerly anticipated.

The Christmas dinner was always a special occasion—Mom bought real butter instead of the usual margarine and we all got to split a large can of black olives, a family favorite that we couldn't afford the rest of the year.

We did simple things like sing carols together, and we always made the tree ornaments by hand. We still have some of them.

Now all but two of us are married. We have our own families, and several of the families live quite a distance away. But over the years we've always managed to get together to share the holidays. And, over the years, things have gotten more complicated—the families have grown and there are now thirty-four of us exchanging gifts.

Several years ago two of my sisters and I started lobbying to draw names for a gift exchange and cut back on what had gradually turned into a monumental feast, with everyone baking and cooking for Christmas dinner. Most everyone—especially the spouses—agreed that things had gotten out of hand. But one sister was adamant. She didn't want to change one single thing about the way we did the holidays. So we continued on as we had been for several more years.

Then two years ago, we had yet another post-Christmas dinner powwow and discussed cutting back.

Tempers rose to a fever pitch and nerves started to fray. The sister who didn't want to change anything blurted out, "I don't care if everyone *is* miserable! I want to do the holidays just like we've always done them!"

You could have heard a pin drop. We all just stared at her in disbelief. Then my seven-year-old niece looked at her and asked incredulously, "Aunt Melly, you don't *care* if we're all miserable?" Even Melly heard the absurdity of her remark, and we all burst out laughing. The ironic thing was, we *weren't* doing Christmas the way we'd always done it—most of us would have been much happier if we had been.

After more discussion everyone agreed to draw names and set a ten-dollar limit on gifts. We also cut back on meal preparation expectations—no one has to bake a pie, for example; we can pick them up at the bakery if we don't have the time, and most of us don't bake these days.

After several years of drawing names, some of us are ready to cut out the gift exchange altogether. It's become excessive—just in terms of the environment, if nothing else. And since we all exchange gifts with our own spouses and kids, who needs the extra stuff?

We feel we've won at least one battle and it's made the holidays more enjoyable for all of us.

*Janet Wilson*
Kansas City, Missouri

## 68

## *What to Do with Unrequited Gifts*

INVARIABLY when some members of a family want to cut back on gifts, there's always someone who doesn't want to change or thinks he doesn't. The key is persistence. If you persevere with love and understanding, eventually he'll come around.

In the meantime, go with the majority vote (which will no doubt be to draw names). Let the person who wants to get gifts for everyone do so, with the understanding that those who don't want to won't feel guilty. In no time at all the holdouts will get the picture: It's no fun unless everyone's doing it. Or they'll begin to see that too much is simply too much. Eventually they'll join the gift exchange and draw names like everyone else in the family.

It's sometimes more difficult with friends than with family. If you've confronted the issue head-on and asked people to cross you off their gift list and they refuse to comply, then perhaps the better part of valor is to accept the gift graciously—but without guilt. If you have no use for it, pass it on to someone who does.

## 69

## Give to Someone
## Who Needs It

MANY YEARS AGO in parts of Europe there was a custom at Rosh Hashanah, the Jewish New Year, which could expand our present-day ideas about giving.

A village elder went from house to house with a bag full of coins. Those who could afford to contribute put coins in the bag; those who were poor and needed help took coins from the bag. No distinction was made between those who put in and those who took out. This practice insured that no one in the community suffered, and it was done in a manner that maintained the dignity of all.

What a beautifully simple idea. Give to those in need. Take only when you're in need. Here are some ways to give a meaningful gift anonymously to someone who needs it:

1. Make a payment to a local supermarket and have them notify a needy family that someone has arranged a food gift certificate in their name.
2. Arrange for a local market to deliver a box of fresh fruit or vegetables to a family every month for a year.
3. Send a gift certificate for car repair, medical or dental care, house maintenance, or other service a financially strapped family might have trouble paying for.
4. Set aside a part of what you normally spend on gifts and donate it to a local family that has lost everything in a fire or natural disaster.
5. Donate blood at your local blood bank.
6. Arrange to have hot meals delivered to a family that has a child in the hospital with a terminal illness.

## 70

## *Slay the Secret Santa*

IF YOU WORK IN AN OFFICE you may be familiar with the Secret Santa custom. Every person in the office draws a name out of a hat and then buys an inexpensive gift for one person who's name she's drawn. At least it's supposed to be inexpensive, but invariably there are those who stretch the rules and spend more.

Part of the "fun" is trying to guess who your Secret Santa is. On the day of the office Christmas party, everyone opens the gifts and the identity of the Secret Santas is revealed.

Many people find this routine, like all obligatory gift giving, is lacking in the true Christmas spirit. Who wants to buy a gift for someone at work—perhaps a boss or a near-stranger—and then worry about whether it will be appropriate or clever? For many, it's just another waste of time and money.

My friend Gail's husband had another approach to office holiday gift giving. Several years ago he suggested to his colleagues that they take the money spent on Secret Santa gifts and use it to create a meaningful Christmas for a family in need.

They contacted a community organization and found a family with two children they could sponsor. Everyone in the office got into the act. Those who love to buy gifts were assigned to do the purchasing. Others wanted to do the wrapping and ribbons. Still others got involved in delivery and distribution of the gifts.

Now the main focus of their annual office Christmas party is displaying the gifts they've selected, then wrapping and delivering them. What a suitable way for coworkers to share the real spirit of the holidays.

## 71

## Create Twelve Days of Truly Meaningful Gifts

WE'RE ALL FAMILIAR with the song "The Twelve Days of Christmas." The idea that your true love would give you turtle doves, or a partridge in a pear tree, or maids a-milking, or lords a-leaping sounds magical to modern ears. The origins of the song go back to pagan rituals, and the message is about giving elaborate gifts.

Rather than twelve days of roasting partridges, buying golden rings, or hiring piping pipers, think about creating twelve days of meaningful gifts that are more in keeping with the spirit of the season. Be sure to include your kids in this process. Here are some ideas:

On the first day of Christmas, give up a grudge you've been carrying against another person. Make an effort to reconcile.

On the second day of Christmas, make one person's life brighter. Greet a neighbor, give an elderly person a hand with bags, or give an employee an extra hour off at lunch.

On the third day of Christmas, rake a neighbor's yard or shovel the snow off her walkway.

On the fourth day of Christmas, take the entire day off from nagging your kids. No "pick up your toys," "make your bed," "do your homework." You can include your mate in this gift, too. You can also ask your kids to take the day off from nagging.

On the fifth day of Christmas, give the gift of good-will. Let someone go ahead of you in line or cut in front of you in a traffic jam. Wave and give them a pleasant smile.

On the sixth day of Christmas, put your spare change in the Salvation Army basket or give a couple of dollars to a homeless person.

On the seventh day of Christmas, take five minutes and send a silent blessing to all the peoples of the world.

On the eighth day of Christmas, fill a grocery basket with simple foods and necessities like bread, cheese, pasta, soap, lightbulbs, and the like, and deliver it "From Santa" to an elderly shut-in.

On the ninth day of Christmas, rather than sending Christmas cards, reflect on a positive lesson you learned during the past year, write a note about it, and mail it to family and friends.

On the tenth day of Christmas, smile at everyone you meet.

On the eleventh day of Christmas, help serve dinner at an eldercare center.

On the twelfth day of Christmas, say a fervent prayer for peace on earth.

The holidays present one brief period of time each year when we can all come together and give in the spirit of brotherhood. Of course, we could do that every day, but usually we don't. But at Christmas, we *could* do it, and get away with it.

## 72

## Create a Meaningful Christmas Without Gifts

I've ASKED HUNDREDS of people what they loved about the holidays. Only one person has mentioned getting gifts. This is not to say that gifts people get aren't valued, but certainly for adults presents are seldom what makes Christmas memorable.

You can test this by looking at your own recent Christmases. You might remember a favorite gift or two, but they're probably not high on the list of things you love about the holidays.

You love the family gatherings and the feelings of togetherness.

You love how the Christmas music always stirs something deep in your heart.

You love it that people who don't even know each other smile and wish each other Merry Christmas.

You love the magical feeling that makes the holidays a time when *anything* seems possible.

It might be challenging in the beginning, but potentially rewarding in the long run, to create a truly meaningful Christmas for the adults in your life without exchanging material gifts. A thoughtful letter, a kind gesture, an anonymous act, or any other gift from the heart will be remembered long after most material gifts are forgotten.

This year forgo the presents altogether and concentrate on creating your own celebration of the spirit of the season, whatever that is for you. Make that your gift to yourself and those you love.

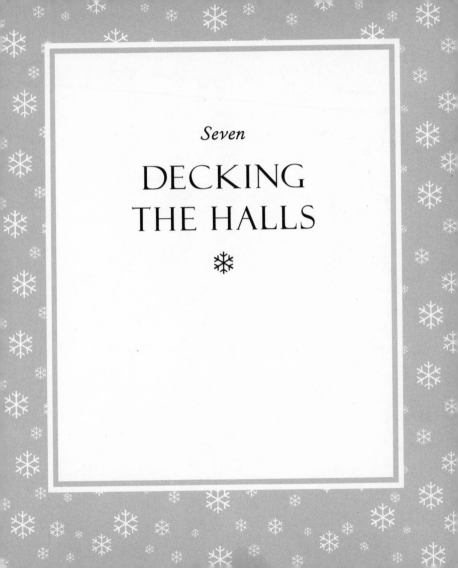

*Seven*

# DECKING
# THE HALLS

❄

## 73

## Boycott the Christmas Store

LAST SEPTEMBER my friend Catherine took a retreat to write and reflect. She reserved a room at a country resort in an isolated corner of Connecticut. The first morning she was jolted awake by Christmas music outside her bungalow.

Christmas music in September? She looked out the window and saw that a barn on the property had been converted into The Christmas Cottage. Thousands of tiny lights twinkled from its facade, and a blanket of fake snow covered the ground outside. By 8:00 A.M. the cars were already lining up.

Catherine loves Christmas, with all the decorations, music, and traditions. But such blatant commercialism left her with an empty feeling.

It's not easy to avoid the Christmas store. There's now one in every mall and shopping strip. The interior design is a contrived attempt at charming, old-country style. The stores are crammed with expensive tree ornaments of every configuration, including tiny nutcrackers, purple Barneys, frosted plastic apples, sequinned reindeer, and matching red and green plastic tree ornaments in the shape of donkeys and elephants for the politically inclined.

There are rows upon rows of wreaths, tinsel, lights, and artificial snow; enormous yard statues of Santa Claus, Rudolph, and Frosty the Snowman; red and green paper tablecloths, napkins, and candles; full sets of china embossed with holly and berry designs; ribbons, wrapping, foil, boxes, and bags; tiny gold beads you can string yourself.

The Christmas store presents itself as a wonderland of holiday spirit, but in reality it's a commercial sinkhole. If you want to keep the holidays simple and cut back on unnecessary spending, an easy step is to avoid these merchants of glitzy junk that quickly ends up in our landfills.

· *74* ·

## *Remember, Less Is More*

SEVERAL YEARS AGO I joined Gibbs on a travel writing assignment to do a story on island resorts in the South Pacific. We made the trip over the Christmas holidays, which turned out to be a special bonus for two people who have simplified Christmas: We got on the plane on Christmas Eve and, because of the International Dateline, arrived at our destination roughly eighteen hours later—on December 26. We had bypassed Christmas entirely.

When we got to the first resort we were led to a charming little *bure* or island hut next to a warm, sandy beach. But when we walked in the door of the hut, we were besieged by a barrage of hibiscus blooms. There were hundreds of them, and they were everywhere—on the bed, the pillows, the bedside tables, the chairs, the desk, the bath counters, the window ledges, and even in the bathtub.

After the attendant left we moved the blooms around so we could use the room, but as lovely as they were, they were mostly in our way. Over the next few days, every time we wanted to do something in the hut, we had to move a hibiscus bloom.

On the second leg of the trip we went to another nearby island. When we stepped into our *bure* there were only two hibiscus blooms in the entire space: a single red flower on each pillow. We stood for a quiet moment, taking in the beauty of this simple display. Those blooms were exquisite, and their singularity made it much easier to appreciate their beauty.

This experience is relevant to the way we decorate for Christmas. It's as though we believe that the only way to show the importance of the holiday is to create an assault on the senses.

There's the tree, pine branches on the windowsill, fake snow glaze on the windows and shelves, red and green candles, brightly colored holiday figurines, stuffed Santas, topiaries, stockings, hanging Christmas cards, wire angels, pinecone potpourri baskets, twinkling lights inside and out, the crèche, holly, wreaths, mistletoe, pine-scented room freshener, and bells that jingle every time someone opens the door.

If you feel overwhelmed by the holiday decor, consider having just one symbol this year. For many people this will be a tree. Others might choose a crèche, or a brilliant red poinsettia centerpiece, or Christmas cards posted along the mantlepiece, or an evergreen wreath for the front door.

A friend of mine who is tired of decorating the tree creates a beautiful holiday display by arranging all her colorful ornaments in a huge glass bowl, which she uses as a centerpiece for the dining table.

A single symbolic statement makes a dramatic effect. Like a single red hibiscus on a white pillow, less is more powerful and quite liberating.

## *Twelve Reasons to Skip the Tree*

FOR MANY PEOPLE decorating the tree is the highlight of the season. But for others, it's just one more complication. "I wish I could find an excuse to skip the tree this year," a friend told me a few weeks before Christmas. "It's so much trouble I don't even enjoy it anymore."

To my mind, this is reason enough to stop doing the tree. But the tree tradition is so deeply ingrained that even people who are tired of it are reluctant to give it up. If you're wavering, here are some reasons to justify skipping it this year.

1. Christmas trees demand time and energy. First you go out and buy the tree and bring it home. Then you assemble the tree stand and saw off the bottom of the stump so it fits in the stand. Then saw the stump again so it stands straight.

2. You haul the Christmas box down from the attic,

carefully sort through the ornaments, and untangle the lights. Sometimes you have to replace the ornaments that broke when you hastily disassembled the tree last year.

3. Then you trim it carefully so you don't smash the breakables, clump the tinsel, or lose the little hooks that go on the ornaments—that is, if you're fortunate enough to find those little devils in the bottom of the box.

4. It takes a lot of work to keep the tree looking good. You have to keep water in the stand—which no one ever remembers to do. As a result, your house quickly becomes littered with branches and dead needles, which have to be vacuumed.

5. Trees are expensive—fifty dollars and up. When you add the cost of ornaments, tinsel, lights, candy canes, ribbons, wreaths, and the tree stand, you begin to wonder if there aren't better things you could do with that money.

6. Having a tree is an invitation to buy extra presents. A tree without packages underneath looks forlorn and desperate.

7. Trees are fire hazards.

8. Trees are unfriendly to companion animals and small children. They present an irresistible temptation to grab, pull, jump, break, and cause general havoc. They are also dangerous if they fall over or if the glass ornaments break.

9. A tree gets in the way. You bump into it, brush against it, knock things off of it. It disrupts the traffic flow for weeks. You have to move furniture around, and there are fewer places to sit.

10. What goes up must come down. Taking the tree down, putting away ornaments, cleaning up the carpet, rearranging the furniture, and disposing of the tree are not favorite ways to spend an afternoon.

11. Dead trees add to our already overloaded landfills.

12. You just don't want to do it anymore.

## · 76 ·

### Plant a Tree

EACH YEAR, over 80 million live young trees are felled, bundled up, and shipped around the country. Most of them come from tree farms whose sole purpose is to grow Christmas trees that are cut and then discarded several weeks later into our environment.

Today it makes much more sense to plant a tree than to cut one down.

Consider planting a modest sapling on your property. Then decorate it with lights during the holiday season. If you don't have space of your own to do that, look for an area in your town or city that could use a little sprucing up. If local ordinances allow, plant a tree and make it your project.

Several years ago my friend Felix and his family took advantage of a local reforestation program and planted a small tree in a designated section of the forest. Now each year around the holidays, he and his daughters make a quiet pilgrimage to visit their very own tree in the forest. It's a holiday tradition they all look forward to.

Another option is to bring a potted patio plant into the house each year, decorate it, then return it to the patio. Better yet, use your indoor plants.

## *Feed the Birds*

RATHER THAN CUTTING DOWN A TREE and decorating it in the house, select a tree or shrub in your yard and decorate it for the birds. If you don't have trees in your yard, go to a local park. You can even decorate more than one tree.

Instead of using fake cotton or canned snow, create an edible snow by surrounding the base of the tree with a sprinkling of bread crumbs and nuts. Wrap strings of dried fruit on the branches. Make balls of seeds, using peanut butter as glue.

Then sit back and enjoy your tree. This is a great educational project to get your kids involved in. You can all learn more about the bird life in your area. It can become an environmentally friendly holiday practice.

In this season of new life and hope, give something back to nature, instead of taking something away.

## Select a Symbol

ONE FAMILY I HEARD FROM simplified their holidays by deciding on a symbol of the season, and creating it together as a family each year.

The symbol for them is the crèche. Each year during the first weekend in December they buy a two-foot-square block of clay at an art supply store for a few dollars. Sunday after lunch they clear off the dishes and put the mound of clay in the middle of the table, along with a tray of simple clay-working tools.

Then they put the names of the crèche figures—Mary, Joseph, the baby Jesus, a sheep, a donkey, the wise men—in a bowl and pass it around so each person can draw the name of the figure he'll be making. If friends or relatives join in, they add the appropriate number of sheep or angels.

They play Christmas music softly in the background and work in silence so they can let the clay speak to them. There are always a few chuckles, and even some moans when one of them can't remember how to shape a donkey, or has trouble getting the sheep curls to stay on.

The figurines don't have to be beautiful, or even anatomically correct, as their album of photos taken over the years reminds them.

By the time the holidays are over the clay is dried out so that Joseph's arms have fallen off or the angels have lost their wings. Then they crumble the remaining figurines into bits and pieces and recycle them in the backyard.

Decide on a symbol that works for you. It might be making hand-painted greeting cards or simple paper ornaments, or even setting aside an afternoon to perform Christmas music as a family. This is not about producing a permanent object that has to be dusted or cleaned or wrapped carefully and put away. The idea is to bring the family together, in a creative and meditative fashion, and avoid the commercialism that often comes with decking the halls.

## 79

## Give Away Your Christmas Box

IF YOU'VE DECIDED you're not going to deck the halls as you always have, it might be time to give away your Christmas box. You know the one I mean. It's somewhere in your attic, probably squeezed underneath a pile of other boxes. Every year when it's time to trim the tree, you drag it downstairs, carefully, so the bottom doesn't collapse. You open it up, brush away the dust and cobwebs, and begin the chore of sorting through the jumble.

First come the Christmas tree lights, impossibly tangled, no matter how carefully you put them away last year. When you finally get them sorted out, there are the ornaments. You paw through mountains of tissue paper to find those that have mysteriously gotten cracked or broken.

Your mother's beloved crèche is missing a shepherd. You remember wrapping the stable carefully last year so it wouldn't get broken again, but now you can't remember where you put it.

After an hour of searching, you aren't exactly in the Christmas spirit anymore.

Here's one option for that box: Put all the useable items back into the box and take it to a thrift shop, a women's shelter, or the children's ward of your local hospital. Or give it to a family who could put the things you have left to good use.

Or pick out the best ornaments and take them as a simple gift of the season to a housebound person in your neighborhood, and recycle the rest.

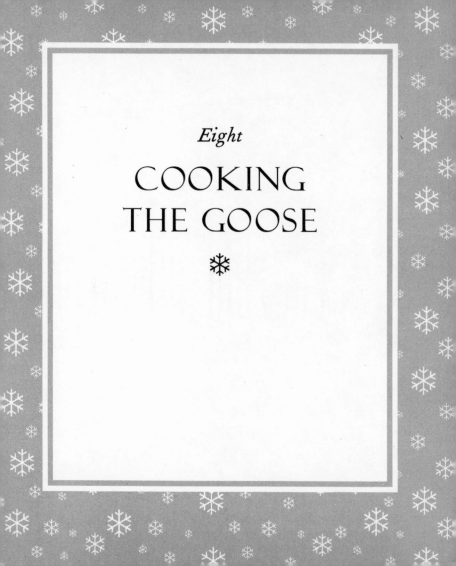

*Eight*

# COOKING
# THE GOOSE

❄

## · 80 ·

### *Eliminate Turkey Torpor*

MY FRIENDS CARRIE AND WALT love the holidays, but they hate getting on the scales after New Year's and finding they've gained ten pounds. Their grown and married kids join them for Thanksgiving dinner, then spend Christmas with their in-laws. So Carrie and Walt fell into the pattern of having a potluck Christmas dinner with half a dozen friends.

Somehow the members of the group were incapable of bringing food for only six people—they were still cooking for twenty-six. Consequently there were always mounds of food and lots of subtle and not-so-subtle pressure to have seconds and thirds. Then everyone would moan about being uncomfortable from having eaten too much. Turkey torpor became the malady of the season.

Carrie and Walt finally figured out that the reason they ate the turkey and all the rest of it was to get to the dessert.

They like turkey, but they love pumpkin pie. So several years ago they decided it was time to cut to the chase. Instead of the Christmas potluck, they have a quiet holiday on their own. To keep things very simple, they order a pumpkin pie from a nearby gourmet bakery for their Christmas meal. They feel like kids in a candy store: they have pie for breakfast, lunch, and dinner for as long as it lasts, and they relish every single bite.

Pumpkin pie has become their standard holiday fare, and their only holiday fare. They don't actually lose weight, but they don't gain the usual ten pounds, either.

## Can the Goose

I HEARD FROM ANOTHER COUPLE who had better luck than Carrie and Walt in convincing the members of their holiday potluck group to cut back. They simplified their traditional gathering by getting together on Christmas Day only for dessert and coffee rather than the entire dinner.

There are four couples in the group, and they keep it simple by taking turns. Each year one couple hosts the group and provides the coffee; another couple brings their choice of two holiday desserts, which is more than enough for the eight of them.

The next year, two other couples take their turn, and so on. They get a taste of the holidays and an opportunity to spend an evening together without the stress of all the cooking and the discomfort of overeating.

## *Forget the Brussels Sprouts*

SOME YEARS BACK Gibbs and I had Christmas dinner with some friends. The table was loaded with the standard Christmas fare. By the end of the meal I couldn't help noticing that no one had touched the bowl of brussels sprouts. Actually, the bowl itself had passed around the table numerous times—but no one had bothered to take any of the contents. Finally someone moved the bowl to the far end of the sideboard, out of sight.

The hostess failed to notice, however, and the next year, they were on the table again. We couldn't pass up the opportunity to rib her a bit. She protested that it wouldn't be Christmas dinner without brussels sprouts. And besides, she claimed, everyone liked them. We all looked at each other sheepishly, then took a vote. There were eighteen people present, and not one of us was neutral about that vegetable: We all actively disliked brussels sprouts.

And even though my friend had carefully handpicked them from the greengrocer's basket, she never ate them either. They sat on the Christmas table year after year, untouched.

I have another friend who feels the meal is not complete unless there are four cooked vegetables. But when she's serving turkey, dressing, mashed potatoes and gravy, salad and crudités, two kinds of cranberry sauce, rolls with butter, pumpkin pie with whipped cream, and apple pie with ice cream, most people can't make room for four vegetables. One, perhaps, maybe even two—but four is out of the question.

Another much touted but often rejected holiday dish is candied yams. Gibbs and I serve holiday meals in a home-less shelter, and time and again we watch the candied yams get passed by. They're okay if there's nothing else to choose from, but when other holiday favorites are available, yams are seldom in the running.

Why do we overcomplicate a meal that's already compli-cated and time-consuming to prepare by including items people don't eat? It's a safe bet that most every household in America could cut by half the amount and number of items served at holiday meals, and they'd still have too much.

Eliminating the items that your family doesn't eat would not only simplify the shopping, the cooking, and the cleanup, but also drastically reduce the expense and the waste.

And I haven't even mentioned the holiday staple that no one ever willingly eats. No doubt many people will agree with me when I say it's fruitcake, and I say the heck with it.

## · 83 ·

### *Stop Associating Food with Love*

A YOUNG MARRIED COUPLE I know spends one Christmas with her parents, then the next with his parents. Arlene's mother does the holiday in a big way, culminating in a lavish sit-down feast for the entire family. Jack's mother holds an informal potluck buffet.

Each year when it's time to go to Jack's mother's, an argument ensues. Arlene is hurt by the minimal effort Jack's mother makes, compared to her own mother's weeks of planning and preparation. Arlene feels you can tell how much someone cares by the amount of time and effort they take. By this measure, Jack's mother falls short.

Jack sees it differently. His family has always celebrated Christmas with an informal buffet. Besides, he feels it's the quality of the company, not the food that matters.

The holidays often bring out this type of conflict in families. No doubt many would agree that a well-set table.

filled to overflowing with the results of long hours in the kitchen, shows more love and care than a last-minute arrangement of mismatched dishes provided by guests.

Others can't understand why someone would wear themselves out preparing a huge meal, then be too exhausted to enjoy it.

If you find yourself fighting the food-equals-love battle, make things easier by thinking of the food as secondary to the experience of being together. Do what friends of mine do every year. Each person at the table tells the others what has made the holiday celebration special for them. If you do this, you'll find that food is only part of the holiday meal.

## Get Out of the Kitchen

TEN OR FIFTEEN YEARS AGO it was quite a challenge to offer a holiday meal you didn't prepare yourself. Today it's as easy as making reservations.

Almost every community has at least one restaurant that serves Christmas dinner. Usually, they include a fixed price menu of traditional foods. And restaurants are increasingly sensitive to special dietary needs—so you can ask to have your vegetables steamed or your turkey cooked without butter.

Check your local newspaper listings or the Yellow Pages to see if your favorite restaurant is serving a holiday meal. But book early—more and more families are enjoying the ease of a restaurant meal on Christmas Day.

Going out to a restaurant is not the only option. Many restaurants and small caterers deliver delicious, "homemade" holiday dinners right to your door. Also, many delicatessens and grocery store deli departments offer Christmas fare, and you can pick and choose exactly what you want.

This year relax, and enjoy your first Christmas dinner sitting down.

## · 85 ·

### *Have Simple Fare*

RATHER THAN MAKE Christmas a day when you overeat, make it a day of undereating by having a simple meal. Have only fresh fruit or fresh fruit juice on Christmas Day. There are so many delicious options to choose from: fragrant varieties of oranges, clementines, and tangerines that are abundant at Christmas. Crisp apples, tart cranberries, and rich purple plums add to the pleasure.

Or you could have fresh vegetables—raw, juiced, steamed, or made into a hearty salad or a heart-warming soup. Include some delicious whole-grain breads, such as the variety of Ezekiel or Essene breads found in your health food store.

Once you start thinking about cutting back, the options for simple fare are unlimited.

The important thing is that by eating less you'll feel better. And you'll be lighter in spirit, and more open to the jubilation of the season.

*Nine*

# MAKING
# MERRY

❄

## 86

## *Nine Reasons to Say No to the Office Party*

IF YOU'D GET FIRED for not attending the office Christmas party, then you may have to go and make the most of it. (On the other hand, if you'd get fired, maybe you should find a company that values your personal contribution to the workforce and places no pressure on your social life.)

But if the worst you'd have to endure is disparaging remarks from people who don't understand, or the envy of people who wish they had the nerve to decline, then don't go. Become an office pioneer and have a gladsome time doing something else instead.

Here's a list of reasons people give for saying no to these often less than celebratory occasions. You can add them to your own list:

1. Expending time and energy on party preparation rather than on the work you were hired to do

2. Looking grateful when your boss presents you with a twenty-five-dollar gift certificate to Land's End instead of the thousand-dollar bonus you deserve

3. Making small talk with someone while balancing a drink in one hand and a plate of hors d'oeuvres in the other

4. Listening to the intimate life story of someone who would never be telling it to you if they hadn't spent too much time at the eggnog bowl

5. Spending too much time at the eggnog bowl yourself, and talking loudly about the intimate details of your own life

6. Being exposed to mounds of tempting, fattening food you don't want, but which you eat because it helps assuage your regret for showing up

7. Stumbling home at midnight too exhausted to sleep, knowing you have to get up at 5:00 A.M. to write the report you couldn't finish because you had to help with party cleanup

8. Pretending the next morning—and the rest of the year—that the accountant never put his hand on your thigh

9. Convincing your wife that the secretary never made a pass at you and it certainly will never happen again

To avoid these experiences over the holidays—or at any time—you don't need an excuse. "No thanks, I'm busy," is the only response you need.

## 87

## Unplug the Muzak

SOME YEARS AGO I walked into a local department store on the day after Labor Day and was bombarded with Christmas music on the Muzak system.

I love the music of Christmas, but I don't love it in September. I found this assault so annoying—and such a manipulative attempt to entice shoppers into the Christmas buying mode—that I immediately left the store without getting what I came for.

As I walked away, I stopped to think about it for a moment. Then I turned around, went back into the store, and headed straight to the manager's office. I wanted him to know how the Christmas Muzak had affected me and that he'd lost a sale because of it.

His first reaction was feigned surprise that anyone would be offended by Christmas music in September. Then he said they were simply trying out some new tapes and they wouldn't actually be playing them until later in the year. I suggested perhaps the tapes could be tested in private. He agreed, and made appropriately polite "the customer is always right" noises.

As I left his office that day I was gratified to see several other shoppers on their way in to complain about the same thing. And I heard other customers and even some of the clerks grumbling about this attempted jump on the season. By the time I made it out the front doors, the Christmas music had stopped. I have no doubt that enough people complained that the manager decided to start his holiday-shopping inducement program later.

Nordstrom's, a national department store chain, takes an entirely different approach. For years it has been company policy to cover all the store windows in plain brown paper during Thanksgiving week. They put a modest sign in the windows, saying that in honor of the season they promise not to start Christmas enticements until the first week in December.

I called the store manager to congratulate him on the policy and tell him how much I appreciated it. He told me they get calls every year from customers who thank them for keeping the Christmas shopping frenzy at bay until December.

If you resent the commercial efforts to start Christmas earlier each year, you're not the only one. A recent survey by Maritz AmeriPoll, the nation's largest custom marketing research company, revealed that an amazing 40 percent of shoppers said they are extremely annoyed at seeing holiday merchandise displayed before Halloween.

Don't be afraid to speak up about holiday shopping ploys that start too early. Whether it's music, advertising, commercials, merchandising displays, or other gimmicks that encourage holiday spending too early—which to my mind should be no sooner than December 15—let the people responsible know how you feel about it.

If enough of us complain, we could make a tremendous difference in the way the holidays are commercialized. After all, this media-induced consumer frenzy is one of the things we say we dislike most about Christmas. We *can* do something about it.

## 88

## Turn off TV News During Christmas Week

I HAVE FRIENDS who are news fanatics. They turn on the TV first thing in the morning. They listen to radio news commuting to work. They watch the evening news while they're eating dinner. They end their day with the eleven o'clock news.

They're afraid they'll miss some major news flash, even though they mostly hear the same three stories over and over again—along with lots of extraneous features, and the speculation, rumor, and commentary that are staples of TV and radio news formats.

I heard my friends complaining recently about the stress of the holidays, and I suggested they could reduce it considerably by turning off the TV and radio for Christmas week.

Their immediate response was not enthusiastic. The idea was inconceivable to them. But they realized that they didn't really *need* to be plugged into the news throughout the day; it had just become a part of their pattern. Then they saw that nothing much happens during Christmas week, anyway. So they reconsidered, and turned off the TV and radio.

The result was this: They had an extra hour in the morning. Listening to classical music while riding to work made them less tense. They talked to each other more. They went to bed earlier. There was a new silence in the house that wasn't so unpleasant. They played Christmas music on the stereo and sang along. They spent an evening making fudge to give as gifts. They bundled up and went out to look at the lights and listen to carolers.

The universe went on, just as it always had, without their constant vigilance. And they had a lot more time to enjoy their holiday.

## 89

# How to Deal with Dreaded Relatives

EVERYONE HAS A RELATIVE or two they secretly wish they could keep in the closet over the holidays. How many times have you found yourself thinking, "I'd enjoy the family Christmas gathering so much more if I didn't have to put up with Aunt Mae's endless monologues, or Uncle Milton's political ravings."

Maybe it's time to take another approach. These ideas won't work for every situation, and obviously no one should put up with abusive people, even if they are relatives. But annoying people can be dealt with. Keep in mind that without a little quirkiness, Christmas dinner could become mundane, even boring.

Here are some other ways to deal with those challenging people:

When Aunt Geraldine starts her usual diatribe about the decline of the Western world, sit down next to her, hold her hand tenderly, and talk to her about her garden. Elicit her top ten tips for raising beautiful roses.

When your two cousins resume their annual Christmas feud, jump up onto the nearest chair and get everyone to join you singing "Joy to the World" in a loud, steady voice. Don't stop until the cousins shake hands and call it quits.

When your father's uncle Drake starts crying in his eggnog about the loss of the family business forty years ago, rather than ignoring him as you've always done, pour a stiff glass of water and cry with him.

When your wife's uncle Sidney shows up wearing a full-length sequined purple gown, six-inch heels, and a feather boa, don't start running to the door with your kids in tow. Tell him you've always loved sequins, and ask him where he got the boa, and how did he learn the knack of walking in high heels?

This year, take a new look at the family members you've always found embarrassing, boring, infuriating, or pathetic. Go to this gathering with love in your heart and the commitment to see life from someone else's perspective. Take whatever small steps you can to ease the burden they carry.

The chances are slim that you'll change them, but you can, sometimes with great effort, change yourself. And when you do, it's possible dreaded relatives won't be so dreadful anymore.

## 90

## Live the Christmas Spirit for a Day

DURING THE HOLIDAYS, we often talk about "peace on earth, goodwill toward men." But in the hustle and bustle of the contemporary holiday, words like *peace* and *goodwill* lose their meaning for most of us. The frenzied way we carry out our seasonal obligations is the antithesis of the true Christmas spirit.

How could you live the holiday spirit, even for one day? You might let go of the anger, frustration, resentment, and stress of everyday life and create some of your own spirit in its place. Here are some steps that will help you do that.

1. When you get out of bed in the morning, step outside. Make a point of feeling the Christmas spirit in the air. Take a deep breath. Carry the spirit with you through the day.

2. Don't let the morning chaos get to you. Don't get upset when kids dawdle over breakfast, spill juice, or can't find their homework.

3. If you drive to work, listen to a tape of Christmas music during your commute. Let the spirit of the season connect you with other drivers on the road.

4. Make a point of bringing Christmas spirit to the doorman, bus driver, security guard, receptionist, and everyone else you see each day by smiling and greeting them cheerfully. Thank them for their services.

5. No matter how busy you are at work, remain steady. Remind yourself that nothing that happens at the office is the end of the world.

6. Don't participate in gossip with coworkers, or complaints about the boss.

7. Establish a policy that you won't bring work home with you. Make your home a work-free zone during the holidays and spend the evening enjoying your family.

8. When you get home from work, spend time with your kids, then have everyone take thirty minutes for private, quiet time to reflect on the day. Talk

with the kids about how they can live the Christmas spirit.

9. Listen more than you talk. Respond to your kids' complaints with empathy and understanding.

10. Before you go to bed, step outside and breathe in the night air. Look at the stars, reconnect with that holiday spirit, and remember how you're blessed.

That's the spirit.

*Ten*

# HOLIDAY
# SPENDING

❄

## 91

## Figure Out How Much You Spend on Christmas

IT COSTS A LOT OF MONEY to pull off the "perfect" holiday. The average American family now spends $1,233 on Christmas. Since most of this is charged on credit cards—and it takes at least five to six months to pay it all off—the interest payments can easily bring that figure up another hundred dollars or more.

*Think* about this: we're spending over $1,300 for one day!

Many people who believe they have moderate Christmases are shocked when they tally up the bills. This happens because, according to a recent consumer survey conducted by the American Bankers Association, two-thirds of consumers have no holiday spending plan and no idea how much Christmas costs them.

One surprised reader told me, "We made a conscientious effort last year to reduce the amount of money we spent on gifts—no big two-hundred-dollar electronic toys for the kids, and we set a twenty-five-dollar limit on gifts for adults. We usually have a dinner party for our friends, but this year we served only drinks and hors d'oeuvres instead of a full meal. And of course we had Christmas dinner for the family."

Even though they seriously tried to cut down, here's what she found when she added it up:

Seventy-two boxed Christmas cards and stamps . . $131

Gift wrap and ribbon . . . . . . . . . . . . . . . . . . . . . . $45

Fifteen gifts at an average of $25 each . . . . . . . . $375

Stocking stuffers for four stockings . . . . . . . . . . $80

Decorations—adding to the lights and ornaments they already had—a six-foot tree, door
wreath, candles, outdoor lights and yard statues,
poinsettia plants, holly. . . . . . . . . . . . . . . . . . . . $205

A Christmas party for twelve with drinks and hors
d'oeuvres . . . . . . . . . . . . . . . . . . . . . . . . . . . . . . $240

Family Christmas dinner for eight including a
twenty-four-pound turkey, dressing, potatoes,
yams, vegetables, dinner rolls, gravy, butter, wine,
soft drinks, cookies, pumpkin pie, pecan pie, ice
cream, whipped cream, and eggnog . . . . . . . . . . $196

4 CDs of Christmas music . . . . . . . . . . . . . . . . . . $48

The grand total. . . . . . . . . . . . . . . . . . . . . . . . $1,320

People often think they're spending modestly because
the individual items are inexpensive, but costs add up
quickly.

If you'd like to cut back on your Christmas spending,
take some time right now to figure out what you normally
spend. Go through credit-card statements and canceled
checks and tally up the amounts. If you pay by cash, recon-
struct the amount spent as closely as you can from memory.
It helps to set up a realistic spending plan for the coming
Christmas when you know what your actual costs were last
year.

Establish a policy that you won't buy *anything* you can't
pay for by the end of the month. Keep in mind that going

into debt for a house is usually necessary, and going into debt for a car is often necessary, but it's never ever necessary to go into debt for a Barbie ensemble, or anything else that goes under a Christmas tree. Doing so is not only unwise, it's truly ridiculous.

## 92

## Cut Your Christmas Spending
## by Half This Year

IF YOU'RE SERIOUS about reducing holiday expenditures, it's fairly easy to see how the average family's expenses could be cut by at least half with just some judicious trimming. Here is one approach:

1. Cut your Christmas card list by half this year (#34) . . . . . . . . . . . . . . . . . . . . . . . . . . . . . . . $65

2. Be creative with gift wrapping, using materials you have available rather than buying commercial wrapping (#94) . . . . . . . . . . . . . . . . . . . $0

3. Keep your family gift limit at twenty-five dollars or less, but draw names with extended family members and set a ten-dollar limit. . . . . . . . . . $150

4. Recycle last year's Christmas stockings. Wrap small food treats—nuts, fruits, candy—and

personal messages, which cost very little. (Or
eliminate stocking stuffers altogether). . . . . . . . $10

5. Skip the tree and wreaths and eliminate the yard
statuary and lights. Instead, use existing decorations on a houseplant you already have . . . . . . $0

   If you have the time and desire, make your
own wreaths for a few dollars. String popcorn
and cranberries rather than buying the high-
priced tinsel and garlands sold in Christmas
stores. Or decorate an outdoor tree with edibles
for the birds (#77) . . . . . . . . . . . . . . . . . . . . . . . $5

6. For your Christmas party, keep in mind that
friends may already be partied out and might
enjoy a more relaxing and intimate atmos-
phere. You could replace alcoholic beverages
and hors d'oeuvres with hot cider and cookies. Let guests know ahead of time that you'll
be keeping it simple.

   Consider sharing the cost by making it a potluck. You provide drinks and let guests bring
simple hors d'oeuvres.

Or, for a group of twelve, buy five or six bottles of cider or sparkling wine and serve it with bread, cheese, and fruit. No need to impress anyone. The purpose of getting together is to share love and holiday wishes. Budget no more than $120 .............................. $120

7. Reduce the cost of the holiday meal by replacing the most expensive items. Chances are the culprits are bottles and cans of soda and soft drinks, and wine and alcohol consumed before you sit down for the meal. Serve a fruit punch instead and perhaps a moderate amount of wine at dinner along with water, coffee, and tea.

   Review your standard fare. Does it include dishes that nobody ever eats? Figure out the cost of items you want to include, set a budget, then spend no more than that.............. $120

8. No need for new CDs. Use last year's. Or tune into a local radio station that plays nothing but Christmas music throughout the week ........ $0

The grand total ........................ $470

This is only one example, but you can see that even by paring back considerably, it still means spending close to $500. Here, it was relatively easy to reduce expenses by half. With some effort, you could cut back even more.

## 93

## *Commit to a Zero-Dollar Christmas*

IT'S POSSIBLE to spend no money at all on Christmas.

Think about what it would mean to focus your celebration on things that don't cost money. Here are some ways you might do that.

1. The most obvious place to cut spending is on gifts. Consider eliminating store-bought gifts altogether (#72). It could be a fun challenge, especially for the kids.
2. In most households, there's plenty of material around for wrapping gifts. Decide that you won't spend money on paper that will be torn up and thrown away.
3. Fill your recycled Christmas stockings with coupons for services and positive wishes for the coming year.

4. Skip the cut tree, and decide on a simpler symbol of the season. (#78). Keep the cost incidental.

5. Rather than buying Christmas cards, send E-mail messages, or leave tidings of comfort and joy for family, friends, and strangers (#37).

6. Avoid the "formal party" mentality. Invite friends to drop in for coffee or cider during Christmas week, and make your time with them meaningful.

7. The traditional Christmas dinner served in most American homes is based on a few basic foods that have been used for centuries, and it doesn't have to cost much more than your typical Sunday dinner. Turkey, dressing, vegetables, cranberry sauce, and pie are not expensive items. For Christmas, however, most people prepare twice as much food as they need, and a lot of it gets thrown away in the name of tradition. Choose a menu of foods that everyone likes, and add one or two truly special treats.

8. Finally, for music, remember the radio.

Drastically reducing your spending is not really about the state of your finances—it's about your state of mind.

## 94

## *Simple Gift Wrapping*

WITH THE AVERAGE FAMILY wrapping thirty gifts, Americans spend close to $3 billion per year on gift wrap. If you take pleasure in wrapping special gifts for loved ones, here are some options for easy, inexpensive, environmentally friendly gift wrapping:

1. Use your kids' artwork.
2. Use comic books or the comic sections from the Sunday paper.
3. Use colorful pieces of fabric from a remnant store, cut to various sizes, that you can reuse year after year. Or use some of those beautiful scarves you haven't worn in five years, or some recycled table linens.
4. Use colorful magazine and catalog covers.
5. Use the art or photos from last year's calendar.

6. Use outdated maps or oceanographic charts you no longer need. Or use leftover rolls of wallpaper.

7. Photocopy a montage of favorite photos or snapshots from family vacations. Have your kids hand-color them.

8. Instead of boxes, use a basket you're ready to recycle.

9. Instead of using ribbon, tie a sprig of evergreen with a strip of raffia or yarn and wrap it around the gift.

10. Gift cards can easily be made by cutting out pieces of last year's Christmas cards and folding them in half, with the picture on the outside. Or, use construction paper drawings from the kids.

11. Be creative with whatever resources you have on hand. Your time and talents are worth more than Hallmark can match any day.

12. Since most gift wrap is not recyclable, forget wrapping altogether. Be secure enough in your selection to let your thoughtful gift stand on its own.

## 95

## Quit the Christmas Club

EVEN THE COMPANY you work for may be encouraging you to spend more at Christmas by offering the "benefit" of a Christmas club. Under this plan, with your approval the payroll department deducts an agreed-upon amount from your salary every week. The money is set aside in an interest-bearing account and given back to you in a lump sum just in time for Christmas shopping.

One reader told me, "I have so much trouble saving for Christmas on my own. Thanks to the Christmas club last year I had almost five hundred dollars set aside to buy gifts." She said that before she joined the club, the most she could scrape together for gifts was $250.

But something's wrong with this picture. The Christmas club didn't help her save more; it helped her spend more. In fact, with the "help" of the Christmas club, she spent twice as much on Christmas gifts as she had in previous years.

If you belong to a Christmas club, consider resigning from it as soon as possible. You can even be an activist and encourage your coworkers to do the same. Make the point that the Christmas club merely reinforces the idea that we are obligated to spend money on Christmas.

If you've already committed to the Christmas club this year, figure out how to cut your holiday spending in half and use what you've saved for some other purpose besides Christmas. You could put it in a savings account, take a trip, or donate it to a worthwhile charitable cause.

Instead of signing up for the Christmas club next year, put that money to better use. Make arrangements through your employer, or on your own, to enroll in a direct-deposit program in an investment account with one of the major, no-load mutual funds. Contact any one of the reputable fund companies and have them send you the necessary paperwork so you can get started right away.

## 96

## Terminate the Christmas Tip

A FRIEND who lives in a New York City co-op building told me that one of the things she likes least about the holidays. is the obligatory Christmas tip. Although it's not spelled out anywhere in black and white, the residents in her building know that they're expected to give at least seventy-five dollars each to the superintendent and the doorman, fifty dollars to the garage attendant, and twenty dollars to the mail carrier. That's a minimum of $220 per apartment. In addition, the co-op budget includes sizable Christmas tips for maintenance workers and trash collectors.

The money itself doesn't bother my friend as much as the feeling that she's being bullied into giving it. She doesn't appreciate the unspoken threat that if she doesn't give, she might suffer their disfavor. It's not just the consequences— a sudden decline in the quality of service—that make her uneasy. She dreads facing the icy chill from the doorman, or having her mail carrier no longer greet her with a cheery hello.

As much as she resents the custom, my friend isn't sure she'll ever summon enough courage to stop paying the expected gratuities, and I can appreciate her dilemma. However, giving gifts doesn't have to be as inevitable as death and taxes—and it shouldn't be as painful.

This Christmas you can start by crossing the mail carrier off your list. Federal postal regulations forbid employees from soliciting cash gifts from their customers. Decide to whom you'd like to show your appreciation, and give accordingly. Then simply refuse to feel guilty about the others.

## 97

## *Make a Contribution*

MAKING A CONTRIBUTION to an organization that serves those in need is a worthwhile way to celebrate the Christmas season. It's also a way to get a tax deduction. But if you're going to give, make sure your contribution really does some good for the people it's intended to help. Being generous shouldn't mean being naive. Christmas is the season for scams as well as goodwill, and there are plenty of false Santas lurking around.

Protect your donation by following a few simple guidelines. Never agree to donate money over the phone, or give out your credit card number.

Avoid spur-of-the-moment donations on the street if you aren't familiar with the organization.

Before you give, find out how much of your donation will go to the charitable cause and how much will be eaten up by overhead expenses.

Call one of the organizations that monitor charities to make sure that the one you choose is valid and you support its policies. Some watchdog organizations include: The American Institute of Philanthropy, 301-913-5200; The Philanthropic Advisory Service of the Better Business Bureau, 703-247-9323; and The National Charities Information Bureau, 212-929-6300.

If you prefer to make your contribution even more personal, the United Way can suggest local organizations where you can watch your contribution being put to good use.

## 98

## Don't Worry About the Economy

FORTY TO FIFTY PERCENT of annual retail sales take place during the Christmas season. One concern people often have is that if everyone simplified to the point where they stopped buying things, the economy would go into a tailspin.

But those concerns are unfounded. As we've already seen, our spending habits have declined considerably over the past seven or eight years, and the economy is adjusting. In fact, it's booming. And the reality is that as spending declines, the market will adjust, as it always has.

When you take the historical perspective, you can see that retailers, manufacturers, and the economy are always adjusting to the marketplace. The Industrial Revolution and the information revolution, two major market changes in the past 150 years, brought about numerous transformations in the ways people make and spend money. And the market has always adapted.

Saying that we have to continue spending in order to support the economy is just another excuse to keep buying stuff we don't want or need.

If we stop buying that stuff—the senseless stocking stuffers, the $1,000 hand-painted espresso makers, the incredible array of gadgety culinary equipment, and all the other purchases that clutter up garages and storage spaces—manufacturers would stop making them. That would be a positive step for us and the environment.

The economy will take care of itself. Given that the average American has less than $10,000 set aside for retirement, the real concern should be what will happen to us if we *don't* stop the mindless spending.

## Eleven

# A VERY SIMPLE CHRISTMAS

❄

## One Way to Bow Out

Dear Elaine,

When I heard you speak in New York last fall about how you and your husband had simplified the holidays, I knew immediately what I wanted to do to simplify Christmas. I was so fed up with the excesses of our holiday celebrations that I decided right then and there that I wouldn't do *anything* for Christmas this year and see how it felt.

My husband and I are fairly average middle-class Americans. The way we do Christmas doesn't seem all that different from the way most of the people we know do it. So I hope my story will help others who feel as overwhelmed by the holidays as I was.

We spend roughly $2,500 each year on the whole shebang, including sending two hundred cards to family, friends, and business associates (I send a personal three-page Christmas letter to all but the business names). We buy gifts for at least thirty people, and our presents are always hand-wrapped with expensive paper and handmade bows. We also buy elaborate gifts for each other and for our two cats—all beautifully hand-wrapped.

We hang handmade, oversized Christmas stockings with our names spelled out in silver glitter. We fill them with all sorts of expensive but trivial items, also wrapped.

We decorate a large tree and attach a huge wreath to the front door. For two weeks before Christmas we have lit candles all over the house and we tape Christmas cards on fancy ribbons to the mantel. We spend several weekends baking brownies or cookies to give to the neighbors in little baskets.

We have at least twenty people for Christmas Eve dinner. Then we spend Christmas Day at my husband's sister's house for a marathon turkey dinner and gift-giving session that goes from three P.M. until after midnight.

I confess that once I'd made the decision and announced it to my family and friends, I was a little nervous. I have always been the social director of my family. Over the years I've made Christmas a Big Event. People have certain expectations, and I was afraid everyone would be furious with me.

My husband was delighted. "You mean we don't have to do the cards? Or go shopping? Or do the Christmas Eve dinner?" He couldn't believe his good fortune.

By the first week of December, Christmas cards began arriving and I felt a twinge of guilt that I wasn't sending cards in return. But I held firm. As the month went on, I felt greatly relieved not to have that pressure.

Since I hate malls I didn't mind not shopping, but I wondered what everyone would think if they didn't get their beautifully wrapped gifts. Again, I appreciated the freedom, since I'd begun to develop a sneaking suspicion that though my gifts were always thought-ful, they were often useless to the recipient. Gift giving satisfied a deep-seated need in me, which I am now questioning. This year, every time I passed harried shoppers rushing into stores, I was happy that I wasn't among them.

We had a quiet Christmas Eve, just the two of us. We ordered takeout food and watched two of our favorite movies. At midnight, we watched the telecast of Christmas Mass at the Vatican, which we hadn't been able to do for ages. We kept saying over and over again: "We did it! Here we are, just the two of us having a wonderful Christmas." We loved every minute of it.

The single concession we made was to visit my sister-in-law's house on Christmas Day—not for the marathon dinner, but simply to raise a toast to the family. And we didn't overdress for it.

That morning my husband asked me, "What are we bringing to my sister's?"

"Nothing," I said.

For the first time, he was doubtful. "Not even a plant or a bottle of wine?"

I've never in my life walked into anyone's house without bringing something. "We're bringing ourselves and our best wishes for the season," I told him.

The moment of truth came when we saw the pile of gifts addressed to us. "We didn't bring gifts. Remember, we're simplifying this year," I announced cheerfully. To my delight, my brother-in-law piped up and said, "That's what we all should do." We spent the next half hour discussing ways to do that.

In examining our decision not to do Christmas this year, the biggest surprise is that it seemed to have no adverse effects on any of our friendships. In a funny way, it actually improved them because we were so much happier, less stressed out, and more at ease with ourselves. We didn't do Christmas the way we've always done it, but at some level, it feels as though we celebrated it more meaningfully than ever.

And next year? This whole season I kept telling myself that it's only for one year. We'll see how it feels, and if there's anything we want to start again next year, we can. I missed sending Christmas cards, and I'll probably take that up again, but I'll cut back my list drastically—and I'll keep my letter to one page. Though it's interesting that in the six weeks since Christmas not one person mentioned that they didn't get a card from me. Either no one noticed or they were too embarrassed to ask.

As for the rest of it, stopping the whole process

completely made me see how much madness I've engaged in without being aware of it. We may host Christmas Eve dinner again from time to time, but I'm determined not to get back into the excesses that made the holidays such a stressful and dreaded time for both of us. I'm actually looking forward to next Christmas to see what we'll do.

I hope you find our story helpful.

*Patti Marshall*
Chicago

## · 100 ·

### *Create Your Own Countdown*

YOU MAY NOT BE READY to bow out completely this year, or ever. But now that you've looked at some ways to make the holidays simpler, you might revise your countdown to Christmas.

Once you figure out what you truly love (#1), and what you don't like about the holidays (#2), it's easier to imagine how you'd really like to celebrate them.

Perhaps you're not even consciously aware of all the things you and your family do each year. If not, draw up a list. Include the things you do on automatic pilot, the things you have your spouse do, the things you have your kids do, the things you have your secretary do, and all the things you'd like to forget that you do.

Then figure out several things you could do to create a meaningful Christmas.

Let people know what you're doing, and then there's no need to do *anything* until December 15—except keep your sense of humor.

Here's one version of what a countdown to a simple Christmas might be:

December 15: Choose a symbol of the season—a tree, a plant, a crèche—and set it up.

December 16: If you're sending cards, cut back, or share the load.

December 17: Decorate an outdoor tree with seeds, berries, and nuts for the birds.

December 18: Prepare hot chocolate and read Christmas stories to the kids.

December 19: Enjoy a Christmas video or make fudge together.

December 20: Take a drive or walk through the neighborhood to enjoy the lights.

December 21: Deliver baked goods to a needy family.

December 22: Help serve dinner at a homeless shelter.

December 23: Make a phone call to family or old friends who are far away and wish them happy holidays.

December 24: Write your Christmas letters (#54). Attend a midnight service, join a group of carolers, or have a silent night (#26).

December 25: Exchange simple gifts, with emphasis on messages and services that express your feelings of love and appreciation. Take a walk in the woods, then sit down to a simple meal that's easy to prepare. Give thanks for the abundance around you, and send blessings to those who don't share your good fortune.

There are no limits to the ways you can make the holidays easier. Decide on an approach that works best for you, and this year delight in the peace and joy of a simple Christmas.

Dear Reader,

Because so many readers have asked for it, I'm planning to put together a book of letters I've received from people who've simplified their lives. I've got long letters, short notes, funny stories, and heart-warming sagas from people around the world who are starting or continuing to live more simply.

If you have an interesting story about the process of simplifying your holidays or your life or any tips on simplifying you'd like to share with others through the book, you can write to me at the address shown below.

I may not be able to write back to everyone—I'm still trying to keep life simple—but I'd love to hear from you. Please be sure to let me know if I can include your name and town, or if you'd prefer to be identified only by your initials.

*Elaine St. James*
Editorial Department
Andrews McMeel Publishing
4520 Main Street
Kansas City, Missouri 64111